FENDER STRATOCASTER HANDBOOK

Future Publishing Ltd
Quay House
The Ambury
Bath
BA1 1UA
☎ +44 (0) 1225 442244

Editorial
Edited by **Amy Best & Hannah Westlake**
Designer **Neo Phoenix**
Editorial Director **Jon White**
Senior Art Editor **Andy Downes**

Advertising
Media packs are available on request
Commercial Director **Clare Dove**
clare.dove@futurenet.com

International
Head of Print Licensing **Rachel Shaw**
licensing@futurenet.com

Circulation
Head of Future International & Bookazines **Tim Mathers**

Production
Head of Production **Mark Constance**
Production Managers **Keely Miller, Nola Cokely,**
Vivienne Calvert, Fran Twentyman
Senior Ad Production Manager **Jo Crosby**
Digital Editions Manager **Jason Hudson**

Management
SVP Global Magazines & Marketforce **Adrian Hughes**
Chief Revenue Officer **Zack Sullivan**
Head of Design **Greg Whitaker**

Printed by
William Gibbons, 26 Planetary Road, Willenhall,
West Midlands, WV13 3XT

Distributed Worldwide by
Marketforce, 5 Churchill Place, Canary Wharf, London, E14 5HU.
☎ 0203 787 9001 www.marketforce.co.uk

Fender Stratocaster Handbook 5th Edition
© 2022 Future PLC

FUTURE Connectors.
Creators.
Experience
Makers.

Future plc is a public
company quoted on the
London Stock Exchange
(symbol: FUTR)
www.futureplc.com

Chief executive **Zillah Byng-Thorne**
Non-executive chairman **Richard Huntingford**
Chief financial officer **Penny Ladkin-Brand**

Tel +44 (0)1225 442 244

Part of the
Guitarist PRESENTS
bookazine series

CONTENTS

Welcome to
FENDER
STRATOCASTER
HANDBOOK

The Fender Stratocaster Handbook is a celebration of the contribution that Fender's electric guitar has made to musicians and musical culture over the years since the company's first Strat left the factory in 1954. Since then, this once-tiny musical instrument company in California has developed into an international corporation and a household name. Learn more about the history of Fender from the world's top guitar historians and take an in-depth look at the key moments in the company's story as they unfold. Find out how Fender's Stratocaster was developed, and get up close and personal with some of the rarest and most valuable Strats ever played and displayed. Study the techniques of the players who made the Stratocaster famous, from Buddy Holly and Hank Marvin to Jimi Hendrix and Eric Clapton. We also speak to some famous players indelibly linked with their iconic Strats, name some of the greatest Strat tones of all time, and we'll also be offering a few tips on how to squeeze the most from the tone of your own guitar, too.

HISTORY

CUSTOM & ICONIC

HEROES

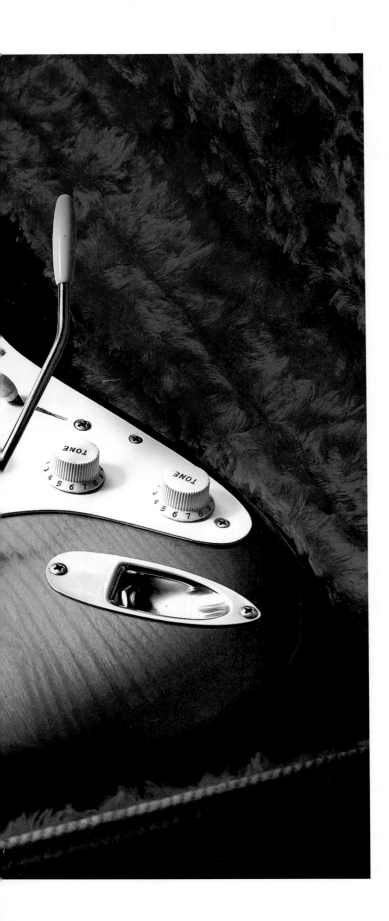

HISTORY

FENDER
the early years

In post-war California, a modest start-up electronics business began cranking out lap-steels and amplifiers for the US music market. Its boss, Leo Fender, may not have been a musician, but he certainly listened to them. His engineer's vision, combined with a team of smart people, a tireless work ethic and a forward-thinking view of the market all combined to create a prototype for a solid-body guitar that would change the sound and direction of popular music…

ELECTRIC INNOVATOR

Leo Fender's company started almost 70 years ago making steel guitars and modest amps: within three years, he had a guitar prototype that would change everything...

WORDS **TONY BACON**

**W**hen Leo Fender and his colleagues launched the first Fender solid-body electric guitar in 1950, almost everyone who saw it thought he'd gone mad. Fender's early amplifiers were good, but a solidbody guitar? Every player knew that guitars were hollow. They had air inside. That was obvious: they were light, and there were holes on the top to let the lovely sound out. Every maker knew that it took craftmanship, skill and attention in order to build a guitar: bending the wooden sides, carving or pressing the top and back, carefully constructing a special box that transformed what guitarists played into beautiful sound.

Since the 1930s, Rickenbacker, National, Gibson, Epiphone and others had made some electric guitars. They were archtop hollowbody guitars with built-in pickups and controls, but (with honourable exceptions) they'd had little effect on players. Gibson set the style for the best hollowbody electrics and had just launched the accomplished ES-175.

Leo, however, was thinking outside the box. In fact, he decided to make a guitar with no box at all: a solid-body electric. Rickenbacker had launched a solid-ish Bakelite guitar in 1935, but it was small and awkward. Around 1940, guitarist Les Paul built himself a trio of guitars with solid through-necks. And in 1948 – about 15 miles west of Fender's operation in Fullerton, California – Paul Bigsby built an electric with a solid through-neck for guitarist Merle Travis.

Leo Fender's new solidbody guitar – at first called the Esquire, then the Broadcaster, and finally the Telecaster – was, in contrast to these experiments, aiming for commercial success.

LONE VISION, TEAM EFFORT

Leo had started his working life in the 1930s as an accountant. He'd been unfit for military service in World War II – losing an eye after a childhood illness – and during the war continued to run his radio store. When the war finished, he ran a short-lived company, K&F, making lap-steel electric guitars and amps with his friend, guitarist Doc Kauffman. But by 1946, he had a new operation called Fender Manufacturing. Leo continued to make the steels and amps, now with his new Fender logo, and expanded into new premises in Fullerton.

Doc had left the partnership because he was fed up with Leo's single-minded, workaholic ways. Leo was an introverted, hard-working man, prone to long hours and happiest when by himself, drawing up designs for another project or playing with a new machine. As far as he was concerned, the fewer people who got in the way of all this, the better.

And generally speaking, Leo was – according to Leo – the only one able to get such things done. Yet he wasn't even a player; Leo took a few piano lessons before trying the saxophone (never seriously), and never learned the guitar.

›

But he thought if there was a product on the market, he could build it better and cheaper – and make a profit in the process. Despite spectacular later successes, during the early years the new Fender company came perilously close to failing. It was Leo's sheer determination and his luck in surrounding himself with clever, dedicated people that would help it to overcome the problems in these difficult times.

Don Randall became a partner with Leo in the Fender company, heading up the sales arm of the business and becoming arguably the most important person in the development of Fender's success. George Fullerton joined Fender in 1948 and soon became what one colleague described as "Leo's faithful workhorse".

Leo's wife was important, too. Lack of cash flow was almost ever-present at Fender in the early days. There were times when it was hard to cash Fender cheques – especially if Esther Fender was late in receiving her wages from the phone company where she worked.

Bob Perine of the Perine-Jacoby agency took over Fender's advertising in 1957, starting the classic, 'You won't part with yours either...' series of ads. Forrest White joined the team in 1954 to take over the running of the Fender factory. He reorganised this vital part of the business into an efficient and effective production base.

MUSIC FOR THE MASSES

Fender's team was now in place and their mass-production techniques at the Fullerton factory worked a treat. There were all kinds of machines, some for winding pickups – Heath Robinson affairs with wheels and pulleys – while one area housed a few ad-hoc finish spray booths alongside a wall of racks for drying sprayed bodies. There were punch presses for making metal parts and benches for final assembly. A worker would screw on pickguards and bridges and tuners, and then another would take over and solder the electronics together. Finally, new guitars would be strung up and tested through a

EARLY FENDER TIMELINE

1946
Fender Manufacturing founded: electric-steel guitars, small amps made

1949
Leo Fender builds prototype solidbody electric guitar

1950
The Esquire and Broadcaster models launched

1951
Broadcaster renamed the Telecaster; Precision Bass and Bassman amp launched

1954
Second electric model, the Stratocaster, launched

Fender amp that was lifted from the line. Most Fenders of the early 1950s came only in standard finish: blonde for Teles, Esquires and Precisions, sunburst for Strats. But by 1956, 'player's choice' coloured guitars became an option, and during the following year these DuPont paint finishes were appearing in Fender's catalogues as 'custom' colours, a label that has stuck ever since. Players began to see Fenders in Dakota Red, Lake Placid Blue, Inca Silver, Surf Green and the rest, but generally declined to hang such gaudy things around their necks. This means they now fetch small fortunes.

Fender entered the 1960s in buoyant form. In July 1962 the price-list included nine electrics (these were the Duo-Sonic, Esquire, Esquire Custom, Jaguar, Jazzmaster, Musicmaster, Stratocaster, Telecaster and Telecaster Custom) and three basses (Precision Bass, Jazz Bass, and VI), with 13 amps, five steel guitars and two pedal-steels completing the line-up. But come 1965, a surprise was lurking. Leo Fender would sell the company that still bears his name...

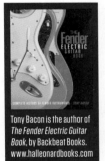

Tony Bacon is the author of *The Fender Electric Guitar Book*, by Backbeat Books. www.halleonardbooks.com

LEO FENDER
PRESIDENT

Fender
ELECTRIC
INSTRUMENT
COMPANY, INC.
500 SOUTH RAYMOND AVE.
FULLERTON, CALIFORNIA
Telephone: LA 6-6625

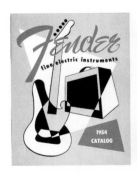

1958	1959	1962	1964	1965
The top-of-the-range Jazzmaster model launched	Custom Telecaster/Esquire; rosewood fingerboards debut	Jaguar model launched	Mustang student model arrives; debut of Fender acoustic line	Company sold to CBS corporation for $13 million

ORIGIN OF THE SPECIES

We put a pristine original 1954 Stratocaster under the microscope to uncover the intriguing spec details that set the earliest Strats apart from their latter-day descendants...

Take a really close look at a variety of Stratocasters built over the six decades that they've been manufactured and you start to realise that the Strat's iconic body shape, as well as hardware and other styling details, has drifted quite a bit from its original form over time.

Indeed, it's only when you get up close to an original '54 Strat that you realise how much those apparently changeless contours have changed between the 50s and the present day. When Rod Brakes, proprietor of Vintage & Rare Guitars in Bath, showed us a very clean '54 Strat in near-complete original condition, we took it as a cue to chart some of the subtle and not-so-subtle ways in which this most familiar of all electric guitars has evolved since the earliest examples appeared. With a little trepidation, we took up our screwdriver to peer under the hood of this elegant first-year-of-production example.

"What we have here is a Stratocaster built in July 1954," Rod explains as we begin our examination. "It's perfectly original aside from a few extra screw holes that have been made in the scratchplate here at some point and a non-original cover over the vibrato cavity. There's a little bit of superficial fret-wear. But by and large, this has been kept in its case for the majority of its life. The last 60-odd years it's been kept away. The finish has not faded at all. It still looks really rich and lush, as it was when it left the factory," he adds.

"They first started making Strats in earnest in May to June of '54, although there were some very early models made between April and March. This is number 522. During this early period of Stratocaster production, the dates on the body and the neck tended to match up very closely, often to within six months and sometimes within the same month. This one is actually marked 'TG July '54', which indicates that Tadeo Gomez [legendary Fender neck shaper] made it in July '54. The body is also marked as being made in July '54," Rod says of the hand-pencilled date on the neck, a hallmark of early Fender production, except in 1959 when the system was briefly suspended after an employee supposedly left some obscene remarks on one guitar's neck! Dating marks were later stamped in ink from '62 on.

Although the prices commanded by rare vintage guitars have stabilised somewhat in recent years, the most sought-after vintage Fenders and Gibsons are still worth a lot of money in pristine, original condition. Thanks to their bolt-on necks, old Fenders are especially susceptible to becoming 'bitsa' guitars over the years, as parts are chopped and changed by various owners, with the guitar losing some of its cachet, from a collector's point of view, in the process. So very careful examination of construction details needs to be made before one can be sure that a guitar remains in the original state in which it left Fullerton. Some of these clues can be gleaned from the finish.

"Often the finish hadn't really dried completely before the neck and body were assembled: sometimes

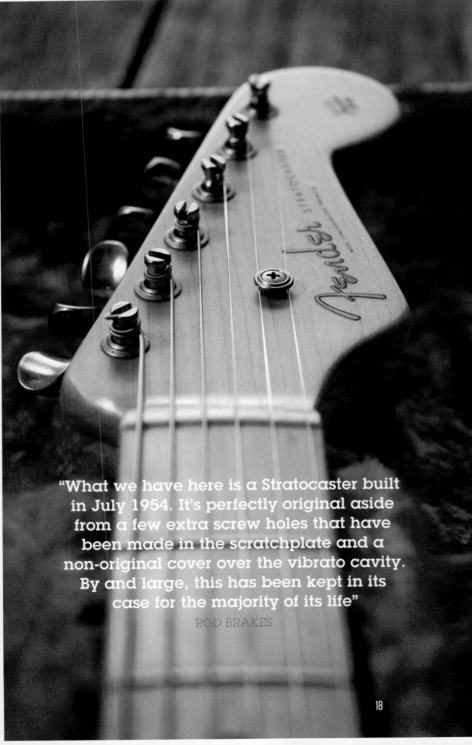

"What we have here is a Stratocaster built in July 1954. It's perfectly original aside from a few extra screw holes that have been made in the scratchplate and a non-original cover over the vibrato cavity. By and large, this has been kept in its case for the majority of its life"

ROD BRAKES

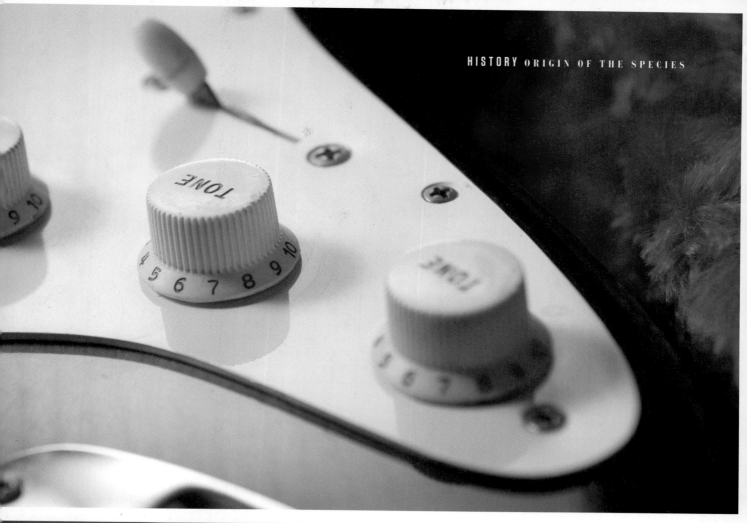

it was still a little bit tacky. So, often, some of that finish will get stuck to the neckplate during assembly: you should see a mirror-image almost, like a fingerprint, on the plate. You'll also see those kind of matching imprints on the neck pocket and the neck itself," Rod explains.

Other clues come from residues found beneath seldom removed parts, such as the bridge, he adds.

"On this guitar, there was finishing fluid, this reddish-tinted stuff Fender used to finish the guitars, and some of that was still visible just under the bridge, under the trim here."

DANGEROUS CURVES

But not all of the signifiers of a 1954 build like this one are so subtle. One of the most striking features seen on very early Strats are the graceful and gently rounded the contours of the body, which indicate the amount of skilled hand-work that went into shaping guitar bodies in the era before the degree of mechanisation increased. The belly carve, for example, is much longer than on later mid-60s Strats: it's less of a scallop shape and has more of a graceful, sweeping curve. The subtle radius on the edges of the headstock, and where it graduates into the neck, is also noticeably softer and is more gently sculpted than on later Strats, like an ice-lolly that's melted just a bit.

"Back then, Fender's production methods were significantly different from what we have nowadays," Rod continues. "It was like a workshop and there was more hands-on craftsmanship involved. You'll see that in things like the edges of the headstock, which are nicely rolled off. That only lasted a couple of years. I suppose when things ramped up, they become a little squarer. It was obviously time consuming to do that degree of hand-finishing, so in time it disappeared. But it's really beautiful."

However, although some of the details of the early Strats were a bit more 'bespoke' than the more workmanlike models that followed in the 60s, many of the components were later upgraded to more durable alternatives, as it gradually became clear that the relatively primitive plastics used on pickup covers and other parts wasn't durable enough.

"They didn't get it all right to begin with," Rod argues. "Some of the original spec details were slightly flawed. To begin with, the pickup covers were made of polystyrene, otherwise known as Bakelite. It's pretty fragile and it looks different from the tougher vinyl or ABS parts that followed: it's a lot whiter and more translucent and marble-y looking. But these early parts are very, very fragile, especially over time. If a guitar has been played even a moderate amount you would expect to see cracks in those delicate materials."

The precise dimensions of familiar parts such as the volume and tone knobs are slightly different from the modern Fender norm, too. "They're just slightly different dimensions, but very recognisable. The selector switch is also a rounder type of switch tip, often known as a 'football switch'. It looks like an American football, I guess. But the three-way pickup selector itself was actually kept by Fender until the late 70s."

Turning the guitar over, close examination of the vibrato block reveals more subtle differences when compared to later Strats. "It's easy to see that on the trem block, the holes are drilled not so deep: the ball-end of the string is virtually at the surface of the block. Later on, they were recessed much deeper. They're often milled much more round as well on the edges there. It's a painted steel block. You can distinguish it fairly easily from later blocks."

A QUESTION OF HERITAGE

Viewed as a whole, the guitar is remarkably clean – so much so that fear of scuffing its glowing finish hangs over you a bit while you play, although as we found when we plugged it into a brownface Fender Princeton, this Strat is harmonically rich and vibrant, while the bridge pickup is almost as ballsy and trebly as a good Tele's. Is it wrong to feel a little intimidated by such 'time machine' guitars? Should we find it sad rather than attractive that it is in such obviously unplayed condition? Or, at this stage in the game, is it in fact beneficial that a few near-perfect examples are preserved carefully for posterity rather than played? It's a tough call. After all, while hardly common, there are tatty but great-sounding '54 Strats around that can show us what a great early Fender sounds like. Ultimately, only the owner of the individual instrument can decide what fate such instruments deserve: timepiece or working tool.

"It would be cool to preserve this guitar for future generations, I think," Rod offers after some thought. "I like guitars to be played as much as the next person, but I think sometimes you get certain [pristine] guitars and... they've gone over the edge of something: it's come too far to take them down the Dog & Duck and start playing in your band or whatever. These things are very, very rare. It's just really cool to see. I don't know what will happen to it in the end."

Thanks to Vintage & Rare Guitars in Bath for their assistance in making this feature

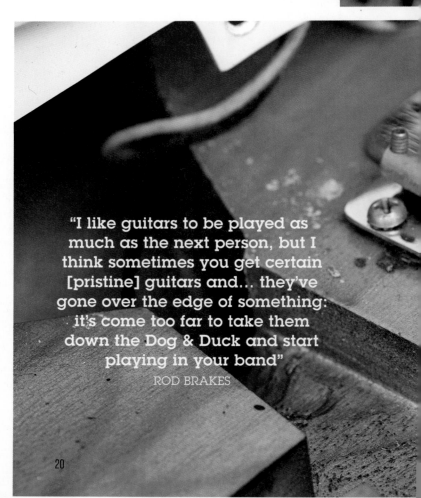

"I like guitars to be played as much as the next person, but I think sometimes you get certain [pristine] guitars and... they've gone over the edge of something: it's come too far to take them down the Dog & Duck and start playing in your band"
ROD BRAKES

MILESTONE STRATOCASTERS

Since its introduction in 1954, the Fender Stratocaster has evolved, diversified and gone right back to the beginning! Here are nine guitars that chart the development of the model right up to the present day

WORDS **MICK TAYLOR**

1955-'58 FENDER STRATOCASTER

The plastics changed progressively to ABS from the previous, more brittle polystyrene; bodies became predominantly alder from mid-1956. Pickups moved gradually from Alnico III magnets to Alnico V, the 'V' neck shape was introduced, then phased out by 1958 when the Three-Colour Sunburst was brought in. Clapton's 1956 'Brownie' sold at auction in 1999 for $497,500. His retired and iconic '56/'57 'Blackie' sold in 2004, for a record $959,500.

1959-'63 FENDER STRATOCASTER

1959 was a watershed year, as 'slab' rosewood fingerboards arrived along with three-ply celluloid pickguards. The 'board became a 'round-lam' veneer in 1962. During this period, Fender's Custom Colour chart expanded, and it's from this period you'll find the most desirable models in Lake Placid Blue, Fiesta Red, Sonic Blue, Surf Green and so on, and of course, good old Three-Colour Sunburst. Famous fans include SRV, Rory Gallagher, Mark Knopfler, Hank Marvin...

1964-'65 FENDER STRATOCASTER

The last of the pre-CBS Strats are often referred to as 'transition' Strats. During this period, the headstock logo changed from gold spaghetti-style to block gold. Clay fingerboard dots changed to pearloid, pickguards changed gradually to white plastic, and the 'grey-bottom' pickups arrived, still with Alnico V magnets. Robert Cray's famous Inca Silver Strat is a '64, while Bob Dylan's Sunburst 1964 Newport Strat sold in 2013 for $965,000 (with all pre-transition specs).

1968-'71 FENDER STRATOCASTER

By now, the Strat's headstock had enlarged, and the blocky black logo had arrived. Bodies became less contoured and heavier, finishes got thicker (both more so in the mid-1970s). Three-bolt necks appeared in 1970. It was all a bit regrettable... except many artists had great success with these guitars! Hendrix's '68 'Woodstock' Strat (sold in 1990 for £198,000 and again for $1.3m in 1993), Blackmore's '68, Malmsteen's '71... those guitars made history in good ways.

1982 FENDER SQUIER SERIES STRATOCASTER '62

Facing immense competition from the Asian makers and seemingly unable to make great Strats in the USA, Fender Japan was established. The resulting guitars were the first Squier Series instruments, harking back to original Stratocaster specs and aesthetics in many respects. There was a '57 maple neck variant and a '62 rosewood fingerboard model: they were genuine Fender copies, by all accounts.

1987 FENDER AMERICAN STANDARD STRATOCASTER

Following years of turmoil, Fender regained its vision and proudly released the American Standard Strat in '87. This was a sea-change: four-bolt neck, 22 frets, 9.5-inch radius 'board, two-pivot trem, TBX tone control – it was a Stratocaster that was respectful of the early models, but also had more modern, player-friendly features. Though the spec has evolved, it remains the staple of Fender's American production to this day.

1988 FENDER ERIC CLAPTON STRATOCASTER

This was the first official Fender signature model that kicked off a highly successful artist program. The collaboration with Clappers took his famous 'Blackie' '56/'57 as basic inspiration, with a V-shape neck profile and more modern tweaks, including Gold Lace Sensor pickups and a 25dB mid boost circuit. EC used prototypes of the guitar in 1986 on the *Eric Clapton & Friends* shows, and it became Fender's most successful signature guitar.

2006 FENDER CLASSIC SERIES 50S STRATOCASTER

Fender Japan established a market for high-quality, lower cost, vintage-style Stratocasters through the 1980s and 1990s. Fender took that model and applied it to its wholly owned operation in Ensenada, Mexico, with the Classic Series. They're the affordable 'vintage reissue' Strats of choice to this day, sitting way below American Vintage in terms of price. In 2013, Ensenada debuted its first nitro-finished Classic Series guitars.

2014 AMERICAN VINTAGE 1954 STRATOCASTER

60 years after those first, history-changing Stratocasters, Fender honoured them with a replica (for 2014 only). The American Vintage Series in which it sits was upgraded in 2012, and now makes the most historically accurate reissues of old models ever produced outside of its Custom Shop, but at a lower price-point. It's a neat, full-circle journey for a guitar that is all at once timeless, and yet ever-evolving.

STRAT TONES

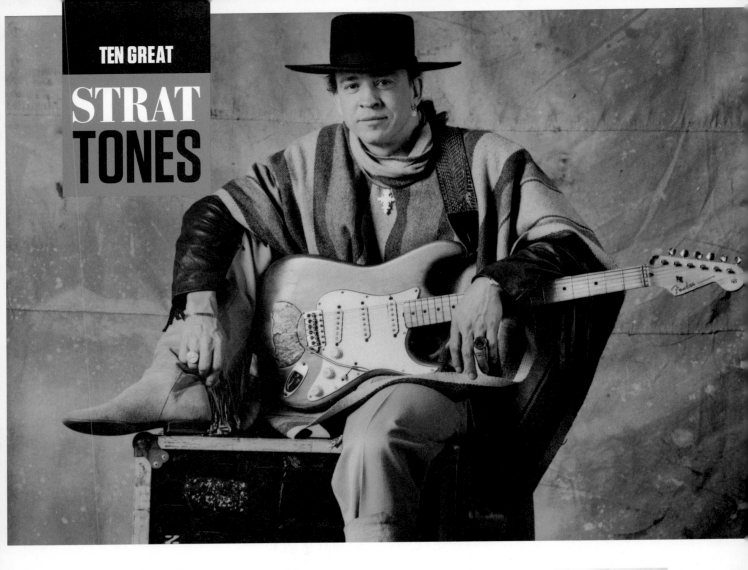

1 STEVIE RAY VAUGHAN & DOUBLE TROUBLE
COULDN'T STAND THE WEATHER
COULDN'T STAND THE WEATHER, 1984

1962 FENDER STRATOCASTER

FOR ARGUABLY his best guitar solo, blues firebrand Stevie Ray Vaughan set his battered Number One Stratocaster to stun, put it through a Tube Screamer, Marshall and Fender amps and a Leslie speaker cabinet, and reminded the early 1980s what a guitar should sound like. Its Sunburst finish was already worn when Vaughan bought it from Ray Hennig's Heart Of Texas Music shop in Austin, and though he'd refer to it as a '59, only the pickups were from that year.

RORY GALLAGHER
IRISH TOUR '74..

2 RORY GALLAGHER
WALK ON HOT COALS
IRISH TOUR '74, 1974

1961 FENDER STRATOCASTER

THE BLUES is about pure emotion, and if you want to hear a Strat player giving their all, *Irish Tour* is a must. Rory's – said to be the first Strat to arrive in Ireland – was worked almost to destruction. Rory took a Tweed Fender Twin on the road for this famous tour, with a Vox AC30 and Dallas Arbiter Rangemaster Treble Booster: a key element to add bite to the Vox.

3 YNGWIE MALMSTEEN
FAR BEYOND THE SUN
RISING FORCE, 1984

1971 FENDER STRATOCASTER

FOLLOWING HIS hero Ritchie Blackmore's lead, neo-classical shredder Yngwie scalloped the frets on his Strat for bigger bends. Named the 'Duck' (originating from the Donald Duck sticker and its yellowish hue), it featured two DiMarzio HS-3 pickups and a Fender single coil in the middle position for his landmark debut album, before Yngwie later replaced them with his signature DiMarzios.

4 ERIC CLAPTON | DEREK AND THE DOMINOES
LAYLA
LAYLA AND OTHER ASSORTED LOVE SONGS, 1970

1956 FENDER STRATOCASTER

CLAPTON BOUGHT the Sunburst, maple-necked 'Brownie' in 1967, while he was still with Cream, and it was used on his solo debut and throughout the *Layla* album. Its most tonesome moment is arguably with a Fender Champ on the title track, which finds Clapton's Strat in equal billing and harmony with the late Duane Allman.

5 GEORGE HARRISON | THE BEATLES
NOWHERE MAN
RUBBER SOUL, 1965

1962 FENDER STRATOCASTER

HARRISON AND John Lennon acquired Sonic Blue Strats as The Beatles were recording *Help!*. Though used on *You're Going To Lose That Girl*, but here's probably the most overt example of a Strat on a Beatles recording: George and John are playing their Fenders in unison, with Harrison's ringing solo; his Strat would have a psychedelic makeover and become known as 'Rocky'.

6 JIMI HENDRIX
LITTLE WING
AXIS BOLD AS LOVE, 1967

1960S FENDER STRATOCASTER

HENDRIX'S GREATEST Strat tone? It's timeless. The sensitive approach and composition of this ballad is majestic and compelling. Which is why so many other great players (SRV, Santana, Satch, Eric Johnson) can't resist attempting it. That watery warmth to the solo tone is because it was fed through a miniature Leslie speaker built by an Olympic Studio engineer.

7 JOHN FRUSCIANTE | RED HOT CHILI PEPPERS
UNDER THE BRIDGE
BLOOD SUGAR SEX MAGIK, 1991

1958 FENDER STRAT

HE MAY have played his '62 Jag for the video, but those tones speak Strat. And Frusciante's reliance on his '62 Sunburst Strat after returning to the band for the last time, shows how much the Hendrix fan values the model. The intimate intro here utilises the neck pickup with what could be an MXR compressor.

8 JEFF BECK
NADIA
LIVE AT RONNIE SCOTT'S, 2008

FENDER CUSTOM SHOP SIGNATURE STRATOCASTER

THE PLAYERS' player proves just how versatile and surprising the Strat can be in his hands, here playing fingerstyle Indian slide on a Nitin Sawhney composition. Controlling from the guitar, he ran through a relatively clean Marshall JTM45. Effects are minimal, though he did use the lusted-after Klon Centaur.

9 DOUG FIEGER | THE KNACK
MY SHARONA
GET THE KNACK, 1979

1972 FENDER STRATOCASTER

GREAT STRAT tones aren't just leads. Fieger allegedly played every Strat for sale in LA before settling on his Sunburst '72 – its finish and maple neck inspired by the late frontman's admiration for Buddy Holly. It certainly makes its mark here on the monster hit he wrote for his band; the Strat bite punches that infectious riff through a Vox AC30.

10 DAVE MURRAY | IRON MAIDEN
POWERSLAVE
LIVE AFTER DEATH, 1985

1957 FENDER STRATOCASTER

MURRAY'S STRAT was previously owned by his hero, Free's Paul Kossoff. It would become Murray's main guitar through a superb eight-album run for Maiden. He modded it with a black refinish and DiMarzio Super Distortions, but his tone was pretty pure here by his own reckoning: 50-watt Marshall with an MXR Phase 90.

CUSTOM & ICONIC

FENDER'S
finest

*Author and guitar historian Tony Bacon
recalls the first time he saw a Strat, and ponders
why this masterstroke of form and function still
fascinates guitarists, six decades later*

Once upon a long, long time ago, I saw my first real-live Fender Stratocaster. I must have been about 17, and I was in a garage. It's a good job someone invented the garage, because without it there would be a lot less rock 'n' roll. Anyway, one of the band (I use the term loosely) had somehow acquired this remarkable piece of brand-spanking-new American merchandise. We all stood around as he opened the case, and there was this sharp intake of collective breath.

What I remember most is intimidation, a feeling that we were not worthy. I queued up to have my go on the Californian wonder machine. I fumbled, because this was a proper guitar and I was not a proper guitarist. But over the weeks that followed, I got to grips with the thing. And so it's been ever since, whenever I've come upon a Strat, old or new. At first, intimidation (oh my God, it's a Fender Stratocaster!). And then contentment (oh, okay, it's just another Fender Stratocaster).

That's how the history of this guitar works, too. If you're at all interested in Strats, you'll know the story of how it came about, and I won't dwell on that. But you have to wait for the intimidation of something new and unfamiliar to go away before the real work can start. And that's true whether you're looking at the instrument as a guitar maker or as a guitar player.

Both might glance at an old 50s Strat and a brand-new 21st century Strat – anything from a budget Squier to a luscious Custom Shop creation – and figure that, when it comes right down to it, nothing much has changed. Well, it has and it hasn't.

Someone asked Leo Fender in the 70s why he thought players had started seeking out old Fenders. He said he understood people liked vintage stuff, and compared the phenomenon to how he felt about his trusty Remington. "I could really hit a target with that old rifle," he said. "One time, I got a jack rabbit at better than 300 yards. You see, some pieces of machinery just suit people." Leo loved gadgets, and you can imagine if, somehow, he came back for a tour of today's Fender plant, he'd adore it. Back in the day, Leo was always scoping for what tomorrow might bring. In fact, he thought the Stratocaster, his firm's new model for 1954, would replace the Telecaster – because it was better and newer. Well, yes and no.

I'm not so sure Leo would have been a fan of Jonathan Richman. Leo's fave was an old-fashioned Western singing group called The Sons Of The Pioneers. But Richman must be one of the few songwriters to have come up with a song about a specific guitar. You can guess which one, right? The song is *Fender Stratocaster* and it's on his self-titled 1989 album. "It sounds so thin that it's barely there," Richman sang of our three-pickup wonder-machine, "like a bitchy girl who just don't care."

Richman was too smart to get into the origins of the Stratocaster name in his song. Don Randall named most of the early Fender models, and he told me that when it came to the Strat, his mind turned to the stratosphere and the dawning space age. He was a keen pilot, so I bet he'd noticed that Boeing called its B-47 jet bomber the Stratojet. He'd probably twigged that Pontiac had a new car out called the Strato-Streak, too. And he went to all the trade shows, so I'm sure he'd sniffed around the Harmony stand and seen the Chicago firm's new Stratotone electric. Nothing comes from nowhere. Even the best.

It was Randall who wrote all the early sales copy for Fender, including their ads and catalogues. In 1954, he wrote about the new model: "For tone, appearance, and versatility, the Stratocaster has been engineered to give the player every possible advantage." Today, guitarists continue to exploit that advantage, wherever we make music. David Gilmour puts it well. His view is that the Strat is the most versatile guitar ever made, that it has this funny way of making you sound like yourself. Assuming you're content with how you sound, that has to be another decisive advantage.

Gilmour was one of the performers at a show Fender staged in 2004 at London's Wembley Arena to celebrate the Strat's 50th birthday. It was quite a moment when he came on with one of his best-known Stratocasters, that one with the 0001 serial number.

Its neck date (June 1954) and body date (September 1954) mean that it wasn't the first Strat ever made. But Gilmour rose above any historical debate and had no trouble at all making his storied instrument sound wonderful. There it was, as clear as a bell at the birthday gig: 50 years of the Stratocaster before your eyes and ears.

Today, nudging into its sixties, the Strat shows few signs of old age. Another sprightly old chap, this one into his seventies, is Jeff Beck. He's prone to nostalgia about the Strat, which he blames for his early conversion to the power of rock. "The reason I left school was because of that guitar," he told me. "I mean, that is brain damage when you're a kid of 14 and you see something like that. It's just a piece of equipment that you dream about touching, never mind owning. The first day I stood in Lew Davis's, or one of those other London shops, I just went into a trance, and I got the wrong bus home, just dreaming about it. You know? It just blew my brains apart, it's never been any different since. It's taken me all round the world, given me everything I've got – just that Strat, really. So it is a particular favourite of mine." Ours, too, Jeff.

Tony Bacon is the author of *The Stratocaster Guitar Book*, from Backbeat. www.halleonardbooks.com

1954	**1956**	**1957**	**1958**	**1959**
Fender Stratocaster launched; official production began in October 1954	Alder body becomes main body wood	Gold hardware and blonde body Strat option (the 'Mary Kaye') offered	Sunburst changes from two-tone to three-tone, adding red to the black and yellow	'Slab' rosewood fretboards; three-ply pickguards

1962
Thinner rosewood 'veneer' fretboards

1964
New headstock logo, pearloid inlays

1965
Larger headstock introduced

1968
Logo changes from gold to black

1968
Thicker polyurethane finish

SYNCHRONIZITY

Leo Fender's vibrato unit was a ground-up creation that defied the conventional wisdom of the day, and became the touchstone for almost all subsequent designs for decades

The vibrato unit wasn't new in the mid-1950s. Paul Bigsby's True Vibrato, consisting of a spring-loaded arm manipulating a rolling bar in a fixed bridge forward to lower the pitch of the strings, and backwards to raise them, was already patented by 1953, and was itself born from the challenge of improving the Kauffman vibrato unit from 1935. When it came to his new guitar design, Leo Fender determined to improve on the designs of the day, and the Synchronized Tremolo took shape.

Leo's idea was to create a fulcrum-based design that was in effect a combined bridge and vibrato. It comprised a steel block in a cavity in the rear of the Strat's body, through which the strings passed; this tremolo block was secured to the cavity via three-to-five springs attached to a claw; the springs counteract the pull of the strings and when the arm is moved, the whole pivoted unit loosens and tightens to create the change in pitch. The design is referred to as a 'knife-edge', or 'vintage' vibrato.

In 1986, Fender began using its two-point Tremolo design on American Standard Stratocasters, where only the two outer screws connect the bridge to the body. Strat lovers are divided on whether this increases stability, reduces string vibration and sustain, or makes little difference compared to the material the actual tremolo block is made out of in the first place. Whatever the answer or preference, the Stratocaster's Synchronized Tremolo system remains essentially the same in 2015 as it was in 1954; more proof that Leo Fender's engineering was built to last.

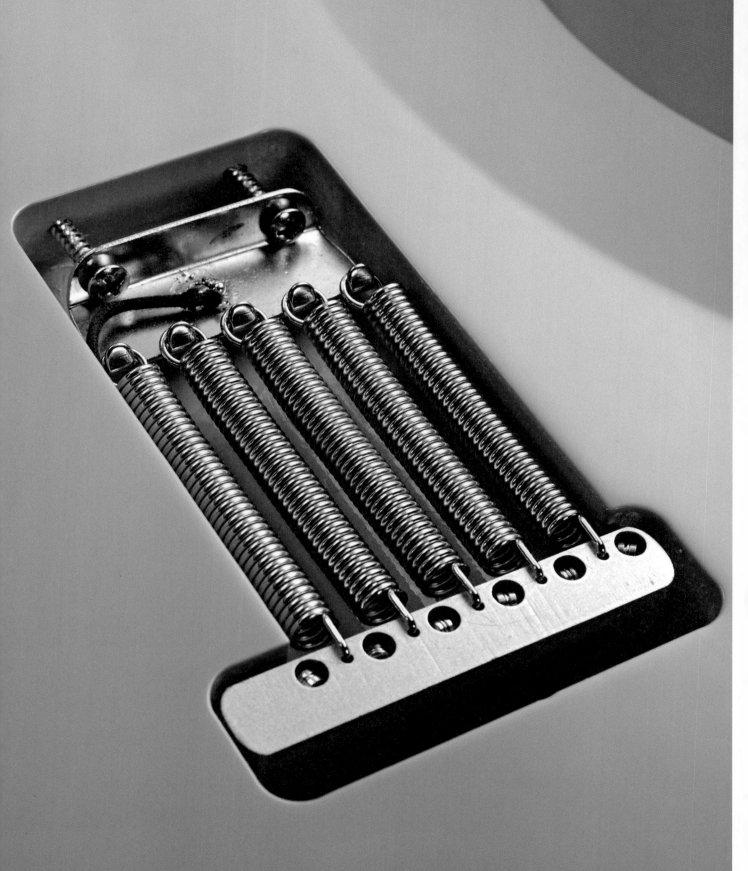

THE INBETWEENERS

The Stratocaster's original pickup selector unit was a three-position switch, designed to select one pickup at a time. But the instrument's players soon had other ideas…

Between 1954, when it debuted, and 1977, when the five-way switch was formally introduced, the Stratocaster's notched three-way position switch was intended to select either the neck, middle or bridge pickup.

Players soon realised, however, that balancing the control switch in the positions in-between neck and middle, and middle and bridge, created in-between sounds that combined two pickups in parallel. The sounds were quite different in character, a result of the combined output of the two pickups cancelling and altering certain frequencies in the spectrum. The tones – variously described as 'honky', 'hollow', 'quacking' and 'funky', came to be associated with certain guitar players – below, we show you just some of the tones of the players who can be found hiding in the Stratocaster pickup selector switch.

If you're a player who finds a lot of mileage in using your Stratocaster's pickup selector switch, then you should investigate models with Fender's S-1 switching system, which greatly expands the range of onboard pickup and wiring configurations.

POSITION 1 (BRIDGE)
Comfortably Numb
David Gilmour

POSITION 2
Where The Streets Have No Name
The Edge

POSITION 3
Pride And Joy (intro)
Stevie Ray Vaughan

POSITION 4
Little Wing
Jimi Hendrix

POSITION 5 (NECK)
Le Freak
Nile Rodgers

1957
FENDER STRATOCASTER

T Although the essential blueprint of the Stratocaster has not changed since its introduction in 1954, Leo Fender was constantly striving to improve his products. Testament to its timeless form, most of the changes that occurred over the years were due to cosmetic enhancements and/or the implementation of harder wearing materials. Be it a '54, '57 or '62, all Strat aficionados have their favourites. But as far as Leo was concerned it was all about continuous improvement.

While the earliest Stratocasters can be identified by their two-tone sunburst and heavily grained ash bodies, in 1956 Fender switched to using alder (aside from those instruments featuring a transparent blonde finish) and introduced a less rounded 'V'-profile neck. In '57 the Strat was refined even further when its fragile polystyrene parts – including pickup covers and knobs – were supplanted by a harder-wearing ABS plastic. Further alterations happened in '58 with a revised three-tone sunburst, although more significant changes would soon arrive.

1963
FENDER FIESTA RED STRATOCASTER

The 60s were a particularly colourful time in Fender's history. Although custom colour instruments were occasionally made to order throughout the previous decade and were offered in catalogues at a five per cent additional cost during the late 50s, custom colour guitars from that period are especially few and far between. It wasn't until Fender brought out its first custom colour chart in 1961 that the choice of colours became standardised and the idea really took off.

The more numerous custom colour finishes include Candy Apple Red Metallic, Olympic White and Lake Placid Blue Metallic, while Shell Pink, Surf Green and Burgundy Mist Metallic are among the rarest. Fiesta Red Stratocasters such as this fine example from 1963 were especially popular in the UK during the early 60s, thanks to Shadows' guitarist Hank Marvin. Indeed, such was Hank's influence at the time that Fender couldn't ship Fiesta Red Strats out fast enough to meet the UK's ever-growing demand.

CREST OF A WAVE

Few guitars are truly unique, as Rory Gallagher's '61 Strat is, bought during his time with a showband in his native Ireland. Pairing the Strat with a Top Boost Vox AC30, Rory went on to cement a reputation as one of the most intense, visceral guitar players in blues-rock history

Rory Gallagher's battered '61 Strat is the stuff of legend. Bought on tick in 1963 from Crowley's Music Shop in Cork, only the wear evidenced on SRV's Strat compares. "There were people who thought that Rory was chiselling it away each night, but it wasn't the case," recalls his brother Dónal. "Rory's sweat was so acidic that it was like paint stripper. After a three-hour set, it was always covered with sweat and you could just see the paint starting to bubble up. Rory was very concerned about it, it felt like premature balding!"

The sweat was such a problem that in the late-70s, Rory started getting tuning problems with the neck. He took it to Fender, who discovered that a mix of the huge amount of moisture in it and the heat of the lights wasn't allowing the wood to settle. Fender made Rory a replica neck and he put the original in his house in London, as little more than an ornament. Several years later, Rory was putting a guitar together and as an experiment, tried the old neck again, which had by then dried out and gone back to its original form. "It was quickly repatriated," says Donal.

For Rory, the '61 Strat was irreplaceable. "It's kind of a lucky charm," he said, "the guitar is a part of me. BB King might have several Lucilles, but I've only got the one Strat. I don't even call it a woman's name. It's what it is. I still play it every day, I just love playing it."

1. Only the middle pickup is original and the tone control has been modded to work on the bridge pickup. The Sunburst finish is barely visible and there is heavy pick wear on the body. The 'Fender Stratocaster' decal has almost completely worn away and the tuning pegs are a mixture of Sperzels and Gotohs. When asked about his Strat, Rory said: "It was the first one I ever saw. It's a '61 model and it has a very flat kind of neck. Although they made the bodies out of Alder and Ash, mine is actually Maple – which is really a one-off!"

2. Rory's AC30 was acquired during his showband days. The Dallas Rangemaster treble boost added bite to the tone. Rory created his searing tone by driving the amp hard the guitar's tone and volume to control everything. By around 1973/74, the Vox AC30 wasn't gelling as he wanted with the sound of the new solo band line-up, so he began to use a variety of Fender amps alongside the Vox, phasing out the Rangemaster from his rig around the same time, although he did go on to use a Hawk treble boost in its place.

THE BLACK STRAT

In anticipation of the release of Pink Floyd's 2014 album The Endless River, Guitarist was taken on a tour of David Gilmour's gear – including the Black Strat that became his most iconic instrument. In this feature, originally published before Gilmour sold the guitar at auction for a record sum in 2019, we explore its storied life and many mods

A t David Gilmour's Medina Studio near Brighton, Phil Taylor, his guitar tech, takes us through his studio setup. Medina is smaller than you may expect for a musician of Gilmour's legendary status, but size isn't everything: Medina is bespoke to Gilmour's needs.

We start our studio tour with what is unarguably David Gilmour's most celebrated guitar – which is something of a 'mongrel'. He bought the Fender from Manny's Music store in New York in May 1970 during Pink Floyd's USA tour. Gilmour had, just weeks earlier, bought his first black Fender Strat at Manny's, but it was soon stolen, along with much of Floyd's rig. Floyd cancelled their remaining US dates, but David again visited Manny's and bought this before returning to the UK.

The Black Strat was first played by Gilmour at the Bath Festival in June 1970. Serendipitously, Phil attended the show as a punter – four years before he began tech'ing for Floyd. Gilmour replaced a lot of his older Fenders in the 80s with Fender's then-new 1957 reissues, and The Black Strat was on display at the Dallas and Miami Hard Rock Cafes until 1997, after which Gilmour played it for Floyd's 2005 *Live 8* show. It remains his most iconic instrument.

HARD KNOCK CAFE

As mentioned, the Black Strat hasn't remained by David Gilmour's side continuously. Phil Taylor explains that it was a switch of vibrato system that prompted the guitar's temporary fall from favour. "When we put the Kahler on, it seemed to deaden the sound somewhat. It just fell out of David's favour when the new '57 reissue Strats came out. So David agreed to loan the Black Strat to the Hard Rock Cafe.

"We were on tour with Pink Floyd, '87 or '88, and went into Dallas Hard Rock Cafe and saw it on the wall. [Editor's note for Black Strat spotters: it was later displayed in Miami's Hard Rock Cafe.] In time, we asked for it back.

"I called the Hard Rock head of memorabilia, but they said, 'But we own it, now.' No you don't! I had all the paperwork that said it was a loan.

"So we eventually got it back. But it came back with the *Animals* tour-case missing, the knobs gone, and filthy. But I put it all back together and put it in the studio." Would David play it? He was used to the Red Strats by then. "David didn't use the Black Strat again until I suggested he try it at the *Live 8* rehearsals. 'Oh, alright!' David says. But when he started playing it again... we suddenly went from that EMG sound to the single coils. That was it. He was back to the Black Strat."

MOD SQUAD

As a close-up examination of the original black Strat attests, it is a much-modded guitar. It was originally a Fender 1968 to '69 alder body with black painted over the original Sunburst. It had a Fender late-60s maple neck (large headstock) and 21 frets, but a rosewood-necked version features on *The Dark Side Of The Moon* and *Wish You Were Here*.

To muddy the waters still further, it later had a Charvel neck fitted! When it came back from Hard Rock Cafe, it was damaged and with knobs missing, so the mods have continued. In terms of prior discography, this guitar features on some huge tracks, including *Money*, *Shine On You Crazy Diamond*, *Comfortably Numb* and many other Floyd classics. See it in the concert film *Live At Pompeii* when it was 'new' for Gilmour, with a white scratchplate.

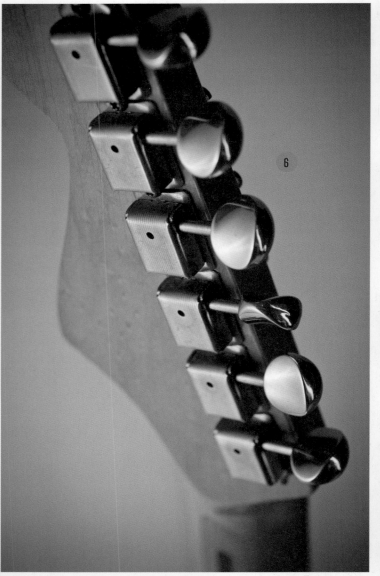

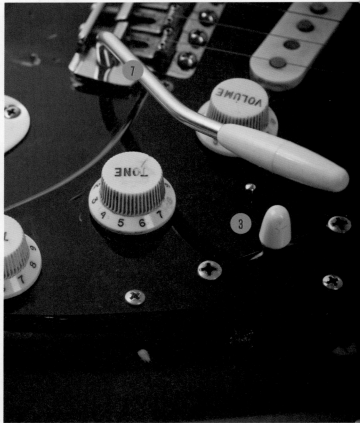

1 Examining the guitar, you can clearly see evidence of old routing work, which has since been filled in for the once-fitted Kahler vibrato

2 In the 70s, Gilmour fitted an edge-mounted XLR socket to send the signal to a fuzzbox then back to the guitar – also since removed and filled in

3 The black scratchplate was added in 1974 and was custom-made, as Fender didn't then make them. The five-way pickup selector (replacing the original three-way) arrived in 1985. The mini-toggle just below the pots allows independent switching-in of the neck pickup "for a more Jazzmaster-like tone"

4 The neck and middle pickups are dated 1971 – while the whole pickguard assembly comes from a '71 'bullet truss rod' Fender Strat in 1973. Meanwhile, the bridge pickup is a Seymour Duncan custom-wound SSL-1C, installed in 1979. It replaced a DiMarzio FS-1

5 After the tonal properties of a Kahler vibrato fitted to the black Strat were found wanting, the original three-spring vibrato was fitted to the guitar

6 The neck is a 1983 '57 reissue C-shape (from one of DG's cream Strats) with 7.25-inch radius fingerboard and 21 vintage-style frets. Tuning is handled by Fender/ Gotoh vintage-style tuners

7 Note the shortened vibrato arm, measuring 4.25-inches.

"Fender make these short arms now, but I originally just hacked the ends off. The arms are screwed in tight so it never 'flops'. David likes to have the end of the tip in the crease of his palm. He doesn't seem to plan whether he plays finger vibrato or arm vibrato, or a combination of the two, but with a longer arm, he may have to play closer to the neck. That would be more of a separate action to David. This is more 'integrated'... He doesn't often play electric guitars without a trem"

Phil Taylor has been David Gilmour's guitar technician since 1974. His definitive book, *The Black Strat*, is now in its third updated edition. www.theblackstrat.com

FIFTY FOUR

Only a 4am start, a 120-mile drive, two plane rides and a European Capital Of Culture opening ceremony stood between Guitarist and a genuine 1954 Fender Stratocaster. Join us as we pack a bag and head on a personal pilgrimage to find the guitar that fired a lifelong obsession…

1108's neck profile is neither overly chunky, nor V-shaped

Threaguitar has always been totemic, to a degree. Many are the tales of wide-eyed hopefuls stood agog at music-shop windows, transfixed by a stringed conduit of wonder and possibility. These days, that shop window is more likely to be on a computer screen than in your high street, but it's still happening every day, all over the world.

This guitar, with its drop-dead curves and near-perfect functionality, has transcended totemic status. In its six full decades, the Fender Stratocaster has nestled right in there alongside the Ray-Ban Wayfarer and Levi's 501s as a staple of 20th century culture and design that remains 100 per cent relevant. Much imitated, never equalled, not old, not new: it just is. You might even call it timeless.

Like you, I remember the first time I ever saw one, for real, up close. I was 14 and our local pub had a band on. My dad insisted I watched them, having noticed the spark of enthusiasm in me ignited by electric blues. "You might learn something," he said. "And he plays a real Strat!" Nobody I knew had a real Strat.

The Aran B Sweaters featured one Marco Rossi on the fabled Fender, punching out Albert Collins and T-Bone Walker licks among many others, through a 4x10 Fender Concert. The combination made noises that stirred something very deep that remains with me to this day. My dad was right, I did learn something, and I'm still learning.

I was thinking about Marco on the plane to Umeå, Sweden, back in January this year. It's probably down to him I was making this journey at all; it's probably down to him that what's at the end of it will excite me more than any rock band or superstar ever could. I know it's not a minter, I know it's not 100 per cent original, but in many ways, that's what makes it all the more interesting.

DON'T DROP IT

Twin brothers Mikael and Samuel Åhdén have quite a few guitars. Over 300, it's said, and thanks to the considerable efforts of a small team of collaborators and the municipality of their home town, Umeå, they've offered their collection up for public display in Guitars: The Museum. Throughout a handful of breathtakingly grand rooms, walls are augmented with gigantic glass cases, each containing treasures that may as well be the Crown Jewels to people like us, albeit way more interesting. They have quite the collection of vintage Fender Stratocasters on display, marking each significant transition in its design; a bewildering array of spaghetti logos, sunbursts, reds, blues and worn nitrocellulose lacquer.

We'd arranged with the brothers to photograph one of their prize 1954 Strats for this feature. Playing it in anger – live or at a recording session – was unfortunately not on the cards, because of the museum's public opening and all the security surrounding it. But just to see it, to hold it, smell it, knock out a few licks; to get the chance to look closely at another old gem and learn a little more, well, that would be enough.

So here we are, the brothers sat around a table in one of the museum's restaurants, having gone to the considerable trouble of freeing the treasure from its multiple-stage security. They're shooting the breeze with the great and the good of the Swedish vintage-guitar scene, while photographer Joby Sessions and I get to work on the Strat, just as we have done on hundreds, maybe thousands of guitars before. It never ceases to amaze me: how the hell did they even imagine this in 1954, let alone make it?

In his book The Stratocaster Chronicles, respected guitar author and historian, Tom Wheeler, goes deep into the many accounts of how the Strat first came to be: who was involved and what their input was in order to present – if not entirely reconcile – some differences of opinion and memory from those early days. It was ultimately Leo's baby, nobody disputes that, and in its debut year, featured a highly stylised, 'Comfort Contoured' ash body, partly in response to player feedback that the Telecaster's body edges were 'sharp' and uncomfortable. There were no CNC machines back then – if there were, Mr Fender would surely have used them – so the bodies were cut on a bandsaw, then shaped and sanded by hand. Ash was reportedly a little harder to work than alder, with a more open grain structure that also required more pore filler before finishing, two reasons the Strat later switched to mostly alder bodies during 1956.

Holding this one now, it's hard to imagine that the solidbody guitar was still such a new phenomenon back then, widely referred to as the 'Electric Spanish guitar', in fact. It's so curvy. Earlier Strats are known in general to have slightly deeper, more rounded contours than later guitars. This one flaunts its six-decade-old

The vibrato has been part of the Strat recipe since 1954 of the Strat were offered back in 1954

These Klusons are retrofit replacements

Time to bin these old things and chisel out a humbucker cavity…

shapeliness more elegantly than it has any right to, even if its thinned, worn nitrocellulose-lacquer coat has seen better days. It's got to that wonderful point where it feels at one with the wood – and were it not for the prevalence of good vintage replicas these days, it would probably feel a little bit alien. You can feel more wood than finish; you can hear more music than guitar.

This neck came as a bit of a surprise. You might expect something fairly chunky, maybe even a V (not introduced until 1955, as I later discovered). It's not one of the very thick, rounded profiles of '54 folklore, but something that I'd happily pick up and play every day of the week. It feels remarkably like some of the modern-day Fender Heavy Relic necks, which is a testament to the Custom Shop's acute attention to detail, perhaps more so to the original design's enduring brilliance: it worked then, and it still works now. This one has had a refret at some point, making it all the more pleasurable to play; a little extra height on the frets makes choking less of an issue on the vintage-style, curvy maple playing surface (one piece with the neck, remember). You'd scarcely know this guitar was over 60 years old, and that is perhaps the standout observation.

AGE BEFORE BEAUTY

The first 100 or so Stratocasters from 1954 had their serial numbers stamped into the plastic vibrato-cavity plate, reverting to a four-digit number on the neck plate from around mid-1954 and onwards. This guitar has a non-1954 back plate, given away by its oval string holes; originals were round, turning oval in 1955, in order to facilitate easier string changes. Likewise, the tuners are non-original, having been replaced with post-1956-spec Klusons at some point in the guitar's long lifetime.

As you can see, our guitar is numbered 1108, placing it most likely in latter '54 (serial numbers were not sequential in terms of date, unfortunately), but along with certain other features, indicates that it may well have been produced on one of the first 'official' Stratocaster runs, in October 1954. A good many Strats

New Old Pickups
Fender's early Strat pickups were typically full- and fat-sounding. Here are five close modern sets

Bare Knuckle Pickups Apache (AROUND £175 SET)
Made by hand in England, these use Heavy Formvar wire, Alnico III magnets, fibreboard flat work and a choice of magnet stagger. Bridge pickup is wound a little hotter (6.4k ohms) than neck and middle.

Amalfitano VS (AROUND £199 SET)
The man who makes pickups for Matt Schofield among many others also does a mid-50s Stratocaster set. You get Formvar wire and Alnico III magnets. The bridge pickup is rated at 5.7k ohms.

Fender Pure Vintage '56 (AROUND £169 SET)
The originator is often overlooked when it comes to retrofit pickups. No reason why: these are more 'accurate' than Fender's '54 set in our opinion: Formvar wire, Alnico III magnets and an average DC resistance of 5.8k ohms.

Lollar Vintage Blonde (AROUND £189 SET)
The US's most talked-about custom pickup builder chooses Alnico II for his vintage-inspired Strat set. DC resistance values are in line with vintage spec, but these have slightly less midrange prominence.

Lindy Fralin Real 54 (AROUND £189 SET)
This extremely well-respected US maker also uses Alnico III magnets, but with slightly higher DC resistance of 6 to 6.5k ohms. Fralin also offers the baseplate option on the bridge: not original, but some people like it.

predate that, of course, almost back to the beginning of the year, even before its 'official' release month of April 1954.

The knobs, pickup covers and switch tip are made from what's often mistermed 'Bakelite'. It has that slightly translucent look – particularly the pickup covers – and is in fact polystyrene. As you can see, our Strat's pickup covers have suffered the same fate as those on Buddy Holly's '55 Strat, one reason Fender moved to using less-brittle plastics for knobs, switch tips (and later, pickguards). By this point in late 1954, the Strat's knobs had evolved to the modern shape we know now, and you might be surprised how white they are; the early white plastics didn't discolour like later variants did.

While Fender and his colleagues were perfecting the 'Synchronized Tremolo' unit, 2,000 miles away in Kalamazoo, Michigan, Gibson was developing the Tune-O-Matic bridge. For the first time, guitarists would have individual adjustment for string length (intonation), but in the Stratocaster's case, that also meant individual string-height adjustment and a vibrato unit. Blissfully simple when you look at it now, it was nonetheless a revolution in guitar bridge design back in 1954, even if it did take regular maintenance and a deft hand to confidently hold tuning stability. Many would argue that there is nothing better for the optimum blend of tone, functionality and feel.

Back then, if you'd chosen one with the new wobble-bar – non-Tremolo versions were offered a little later – you'd have had to fork out $249.50. The case was $39.95 extra, and: "of hardshell construction, crushed-plush lined... covered in a grain hair seal, simulated leather covering", no less. The average US wage in 1954 was around $3,000, so a Strat would have been around a month's wages.

FOREVER YOUNG

What did we learn on our trip to Umeå to see what its owners laughingly call this "old, dusty guitar"? Are we just perpetuating a vintage myth that has no relevance in modern music? I don't think so. What's really astonishing about this guitar is that even over six decades after it was first designed and made, you could chuck it in a gigbag, go and do tonight's gig and treat it like any other decent Stratocaster that has ever existed. Perhaps we shouldn't be too surprised, because however revolutionary, the Strat's near-perfect blend of form and function lies right at the heart of its many other ostensible contradictions: versatile yet simple; futuristic yet timeless; workaday yet remarkable; all different, yet all strangely the same. Above all, it's a guitar that you dream about, yet one which you can just go out and buy with a few hundred quid... as long as you don't want this original '54, of course!

Around mid-1954, Strat serial numbers began to be stamped onto the neckplates

The '54 is one of many stunning guitars on show at Mikael and Samuel Ahdén's museum

1 Serial number
The earliest Strats – around 100 or so instruments – had their serial numbers on the plastic backplates. Mid-1954, it became a four-digit number on the neck plate. (Five from 1955, though four-digit numbers still exist into 1956!)

2 Headstock
1954 and early '55 Strats had a softer radius to the headstock edges than later models, where the edges became 'sharper'. Patent numbers weren't added to the decals until 1961

3 Plastics
Fender's plastics went through various transitions: early Strats used a very brittle material (polystyrene, often referred to as 'Bakelite'), that was phased out during 1956 and 1957. Pickguards, knobs, pickup covers and switch tips all changed shape/profile during that time, too

4 Vibrato
Fender's original 'Synchronized Tremolo' has remained unchanged (although other variants have been developed) in 60+ years. Early saddles were stamped with 'FENDER' on one side and 'PAT. PEND.' on the other

5 Pickup Selector
Five-way switches weren't introduced officially until 1976/77, but players worked out almost instantly that you could find unusual and usable sounds with the three-way 'jammed' between main settings

6 Body
Ash was the first body of timber for Strats, and was often a single piece or two pieces on early models. Alder became the standard body wood during 1956, with ash retained for the blonde colour option

7 Neck
All Stratocaster necks were a single piece of maple, including the fingerboard, right up until 1959, when separate rosewood fingerboards were introduced

CLAPTON'S 'BLACKIE' STRATOCASTER

Back in 2006, the Fender Custom Shop recreated Eric Clapton's most famous guitar with painstaking accuracy for a limited run. Here's the story of the original instrument, and how Fender went about recreating it...

PHOTOGRAPHY **MATTHEW WORDEN**

Eddie Van Halen's Frankenstein, Billy Gibbons' Pearly Gates, Brian May's Red Special... a pet name certainly helps if you want your unique guitar to exude a special aura. And there are no more mojo-laden axes than Eric Clapton's Blackie. Partly because this is no off-the-shelf old Strat.

Back in 1970, Clapton was a member of short-lived supergroup Blind Faith, and mostly playing Gibsons – Les Pauls, ES-335s, SGs and Firebirds. However, impressed by bandmate Steve Winwood's performance with a Stratocaster, Clapton visited Nashville's small Sho-Bud guitar shop mid-tour in 1970, in search of new wood to fire his muse. Once there, he found a rack of six second-hand Fender Strats and bought the lot for a bargain $100 each. Three were given to close friends – Winwood, George Harrison and Pete Townshend – while the other three were dismantled to build a hybrid.

Clapton began by selecting a '56 alder body, finished in black nitro-cellulose lacquer. The neck came from a '57, one-piece maple with a hard 'V' contour he loved, while pickups and hardware from the three source guitars were selected and fitted. Blackie was born – it was a mongrel guitar for a pedigree player.

It was EC's main guitar from 1973 to the mid-80s. He debuted it at the Rainbow Concert of '73. It was used to record *Cocaine*, *Wonderful Tonight*, *I Shot The Sheriff* and *Lay Down Sally* among other hits. It's there on the cover of his 1977 album, *Slowhand*. He played it at 1985's *Live Aid*. It was eventually retired from work in 1987 – replaced by Fender's Eric Clapton Signature model, which was ergonomically based on Blackie itself. Clapton brought Blackie out of its retirement for one song in 1991 at the Royal Albert Hall, but the real news happened when he held the second of his Crossroads charity guitar auctions, in June 2004. Many were astonished he'd even offer the guitar for sale. Eyebrows raised further when Blackie was bought by US retailers Guitar Center for a staggering $959,500, entering the record books as the most expensive guitar ever to have been sold at auction... A record it still holds.

Fast forward to 2006, and the Fender Custom Shop built a very limited run of exact Blackie Tribute models, which will hit a very few select dealers from November. Every detail has been diligently replicated, from the worn- to-the-wood body, to the weathered neck, to the unmistakeable cigarette burns on the headstock. Of course, they were only 'available' if you had a huge amount of cash (UK RRP was £13,879!), and if you were lucky (just 60 left the USA).

But if nothing else, these Blackie Tribute guitars were a triumph of cloning a legendary rock artefact. Clapton has twanged his approval of the Tributes: he played what looked like Blackie on three songs at his Royal Albert Hall gig in 2006, but it was in fact the prototype of this homage.

When they visited the UK, the Fender Custom Shop's Mike Eldred and Todd Krause exclusively told *Guitarist* how they recreated an icon...

What access did Fender have?

MIKE ELDRED: "We've spec'd the guitar twice. Todd had access before any other builder. The original Blackie's in good shape. It's all been properly shielded on the inside. The wiring has been tidied up a little bit since the last time we'd seen it. There was shielding tape on the inside and Electrodag conductive paint. But the guitar was still very playable."

TODD KRAUSE: "It was well maintained. Lee Dickson [Eric's guitar tech] didn't hesitate about taking out a rusted pickguard screw and replacing it with a new one. The pickups have been rewired. The saddles on the bridge have been switched. Springs and screws that were too rusty to adjust have been replaced with new ones. Lee has probably dressed the frets several times. The neck refin was professional, though there's not much paint [lacquer] left! It was treated as a tool but wasn't neglected, it was cleaned and kept right."

You say the neck has been shaped by Eric's hand: is the wear so considerable that it's actually changed the shape a little?

ME: "I think it has, because he played that guitar so much and the amount of wear, certainly around the edges on the fretboard... That happens from playing the crap out of the guitar. That's what we mean."

Is there anything unusual about Blackie?

TK: "Yes, and the thing about each Tribute model that we do is that there are always new techniques for ageing that we have to come up with. I had to come up with some new techniques as well as pull from our tried-and-tested methods. For example, the wear on Blackie's fingerboard: we've done necks with divets all over the fingerboard, some a lot, but as far as I know we've never done a neck where there's more finish off than on. Because the neck had been reworked and refinished, when you sand lacquer off, or when it wears off, sweat gets under the paint and it greys the wood. That's something we reproduce when we do a Relic neck. But this had been refinished so this was under the finish. When you take a piece of wood like that to refinish it, you sand it up clean, but the sweat has soaked into the grain and it leaves these little dark whiskers with the finish over it. We had to finish a neck, then un-finish it, then refinish it, then wear it out! There was trial and error involved, but I think it's pretty spot on."

ME: "When we do the replication process on a Tribute guitar, part of the job is to be a detective. How did the guitar get like this? Why is there dirt under the lacquer? Todd had to reverse-engineer what it had been through in the refinishing process, as the body had been refinished, too."

TK: "Blackie will be an inspiration on our future Relics. Now I have new techniques that I can put into future Relics..."

The shots in this feature are of Clapton's original. See www.fender.com for more on the creation of the Custom Shop Tribute model

STEVIE RAY VAUGHAN'S 'LENNY'

This CBS-era Stratocaster was a favourite squeeze of Stevie Ray Vaughan, and he used it for his most evocative performances and the recordings of two of his most memorable tunes

This circa-1965 Stratocaster belonged to Stevie Ray Vaughan, and was nicknamed 'Lenny' by him in honour of his wife, Lenora. He turned to it when performing live to play the song *Lenny*, a mesmerising, dream-like, jazz-inflected instrumental with a dynamic clean tone quite in contrast to the full-throttle Texas blues that was his stock-in-trade. The guitarist would often close the set by performing the song sitting on the stage edge, smoking a cigarette contemplatively and conjuring magical, fluid runs and extended chords from his fretboard that were suspended somewhere between Hendrix's *Little Wing* and the flash of Kenny Burrell, two of Stevie Ray's major inspirations.

A circa 1965-model Strat found in a pawn shop in the early 1980s, 'Lenny' was a heavily modded creation. Its Sunburst finish had been removed and a dark lacquer applied in its place; a tortoiseshell inlay believed to be a pickguard from an early-1900s mandolin was inlaid in its body; and Stevie replaced its rosewood neck with a maple neck given to him by Billy Gibbons. It was sold at auction at Christie's in 2004 for $623,500; Fender's Custom Shop created a limited run of 235 replicas in 2007.

Master builder Jason Smith with an SRV 'Lenny' Strat

Lenny bookended Stevie Ray's recording career. It was used to record *Lenny* on debut album, *Texas Flood* (1983), and for *Riviera Paradise*, the closing song on his final studio album, *In Step*, in 1989. If you've ever doubted the Stratocaster's powers of expression, we urge you to give both a listen.

FENDER BILLY CORGAN STRATOCASTER

Smashing or pumpkin? Let's hope Corgan's signature axe isn't a Billy-no-mates

He's big. He's bald. He wears a floor-length leather dress and has hands that would beat a mountain gorilla at thumb war. Throw in a pathological hatred for imperfection and dubious 'people skills', and it must have been a tense afternoon in the Fender Custom Shop when Smashing Pumpkins leader Billy Corgan swung by to oversee his signature Strat. God knows how many prototypes later, it's passed the white-glove test of alt rock's hardest taskmaster. It's good enough for him, but is it good enough for us?

The sizzle: Cynics say signatures are all about the fret inlays. Well, screw the cynics; Corgan has got stuck in under the bonnet. "It's not geeked out in a way that only I could be interested in," says Bill of the understated visuals. And faced with the traditional alder body and time-honoured maple bolt-neck, you'd have to nod in agreement. Let's be honest – it's a Stratocaster, really, isn't it?

"It's sort of a standard Fender guitar," he agrees. "I've just hot-rodded up some of the aspects. We have a hard-tail bridge on the back for better sustain, and a heavier body weight so there's enough low end in the guitar. I've been working with DiMarzio to find a pickup that's got both Strat articulation [and] enough low-end heavy metal to get the Sabbath that I want. A lot of people do endorsements but don't really play the guitars. I'm playing this guitar every night."

We say: Billy Corgan's Strat rocks the house. Sure, the stock body is boring, but the ergonomic contours hammer home the argument that the Strat is still the world's most comfortable design. We've played faster

necks, but the modern C-profile on this one is satisfying and chunky, without necessitating goalkeeper hands. One thing we can't excuse is the lack of vibrato, but this guitar is £100 less than a 'normal' US Strat.

And so to those DiMarzios. Corgan's mission to develop a high-gain Strat is admirable, and open-minded guitarists will surely agree he's achieved his goal. While there's not a significant boost in sustain to this reviewer's ears, Corgan's bespoke neck and bridge humbuckers (with DiMarzio's Chopper in the middle) bring a depth and snarl that's perfect for nailing harder Pumpkin moments like Bullet With Butterfly Wings, or bolting balls to your own alt-rock classics. As a Strat, it's adaptable too, and what seals the deal is the glassy, classy shimmer when you ditch the gain, combine the neck and middle pickups and break into 1979.

This isn't for Stratocaster purists (it doesn't offer the classic 'Hendrix' singlecoil sound that defines the model), nor is it really for Corgan nuts (you wouldn't know it was his if we hadn't told you). But if you crave a model that tweaks the nose of the Stratocatser format and rocks the roof off in the process, this demands investigation.

AT A GLANCE

Fender Billy Corgan Stratocaster

BODY: Solid alder

NECK: Maple, bolt-on

FINGERBOARD: Maple with dot inlays

SCALE: 25.5"

FRETS: 22

PICKUPS: 2x DiMarzio Billy Corgan humbuckers, DiMarzio Chopper

CONTROLS: Volume, 2x tone, 5-way pickup selector

HARDWARE: Chrome

LEFT HANDED: No

FINISH: Olympic White (pictured), Flat Black

CONTACT: Fender GBI 01342 331700

WEB: www.fender.co.uk

"Corgan's bespoke neck and bridge pickups are perfect for pumpkins moments and your own alt rock classics"

SUMMARY

For: Bags of attitude and killer feel

Against: No vibrato or visual whimsy

★★★★☆

We say... Smashing stuff

1 Body
As a lifelong Strat devotee, Billy has left that iconic doublecut body untouched

2 Pickups
With DiMarzio's Billy Corgan humbuckers at the neck and bridge, this axe shakes the practice room

3 Selector
A traditional five-way pickup selector gives wide scope for different tonalities

4 Bridge
The thru-bridge is convenient but the lack of a vibrato is still a kick in the teeth

THE HITMAKER

With an estimated $2 billion-worth of music having featured his golden-era 1960 Stratocaster, Chic legend Nile Rodgers is the King Midas of pop. Guitarist caught up with him around the time of Daft Punk's mega-hit Get Lucky, featuring Rodgers' funky guitar lines, to ask him about his signature Fender

**e read that $2 billion-worth of music has flowed through the Hitmaker….**
"Yeah, and that was an estimate some time ago, so you add on a couple of years. You gotta realise how much music I play. When you think about it, people know the Chic hits and they know *Get Lucky*, but they don't realise about the film scores, the video games, all that other stuff. You add all that together, it becomes a pretty sizeable number rather quickly.

"So that $2 billion number… I think I heard that three years ago. Maybe even longer. I've been regurgitating that fact for a long time now!"

What would you say makes the Hitmaker such a special Strat?
"It's lighter than any other Strat. Fender bought a shipment of alder around 1957. They paid a really low price for this wood, and it was non-delivery, so all they had to do was go pick it up. But when they got there, they discovered the wood was grown up on a mountain. So they bring it all back to California and they realised wood that's not grown at sea level is dryer and lighter. So they think, 'Okay, let's use this, but we'll never use it again, 'cos it's too expensive.' So my body is alder and my neck is maple."

You've tweeted about designing a signature Fender Strat. How's that going?
"We are doing it as we speak. About three weeks ago, I tried the latest body configuration, and I said, 'Well, guys, it's back to the drawing board – again.' We've been working on it for years. It's gonna sound like the Hitmaker. We've copied it exactly. We had to. That's what we finally had to agree to do, no matter how [much hassle it was]. The guys at Fender are really smart: they know what most people like. I understand that, but I had to convince them that if you really want this guitar, you have to make this guitar."

What pickups are being fitted to the signature?
"Just the [standard] Fender pickups, wound right there at the factory. They've got the outputs exactly the same as the Hitmaker. They just sent me three different pickups. When we put all three of their pickups with my body, one of them sounds identical. The other is close, in a way I like a lot. One of them, forget about it, it doesn't work at all. I think they may have been trying to trick me. They were gonna give me these really cool, hype pickups that everybody likes, but it's like, 'Nah, that ain't it.' I'm not saying it's not a good sound, I'm saying it's not *this* sound."

The limited-edition Custom Shop Nile Rodgers Hitmaker Strat was unveiled at NAMM 2014

EXCLUSIVE OFFER!

SAVE MONEY ON THE COVER PRICE

NEVER MISS AN ISSUE

DIRECT TO YOUR DOOR & DIGITAL DEVICE

ONLY £5* FOR ISSUES

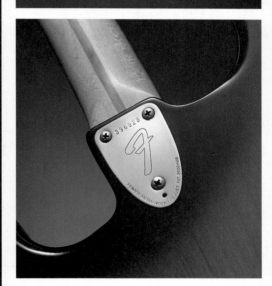

THE CBS STRAT

The Stratocaster of the mid-60s onwards underwent a series of modifications that strayed from previous designs, and these – together with the worsening quality of Fender's output – saw them almost universally damned as inferior instruments to their forbears

1 The first CBS Stratocasters had an enlarged headstock from 1965, a black logo from 1968 and chrome-plated Fender tuners from 1967

2 CBS-era Strats introduced thick polyester undercoat in the late-60s because they were easier to work with

3 In 1970, Leo Fender – who remained a consultant to CBS – came up with the 'Tilt Neck' system to enable easier truss-rod adjustment. The truss-rod adjuster became a bullet-shaped protrusion at the headstock. The system was brought into production 1971, and the four-bolt neck was replaced with a three-bolt attachment at this time

4 The 1970s vibrato mechanism became a one-piece die-cast baseplate and bar, instead of the separate steel components on earlier models, and die-cast saddles replaced the earlier steel ones

5 From 1974, staggered polepieces were replaced with straight-line polepieces. Changes in pickup production also led to some pickups being microphonic

6 In 1977, the three-way pickup selector was replaced with a five-way unit for 'inbetween' tones

1962 FENDER STRATOCASTER

The Stratocaster's fretboard changed in 1962, at a time when the model was enjoying international popularity in all kinds of emerging musical genres

The dawn of the 60s ushered in a decade of change for Fender, while the Stratocaster's popularity was soaring thanks to the likes of The Beach Boys, Dick Dale and Hank Marvin. Even before the takeover by CBS in 1965, the Strat underwent a number of significant changes, perhaps most notably in the fretboard department. From 1959, a 'slab' rosewood 'board with the underside milled flat was standard. During 1962, Fender switched to pre-radius'd maple necks fitted with a uniform width 'round laminate' rosewood cap that followed the curve.

This gorgeous example features the earlier slab arrangement; the shape of the rosewood section behind the nut is a dead giveaway. The other key indicator as to this Strat's age is the green-hued scratchplate, a result of the three-ply white/black/white celluloid nitrate pickguard's centre section bleeding into the other layers. Shrinkage over time often leads to cracking around the neck pickup's bass-side screw, too, also seen here. These 'guards were replaced in 1965, but there's something magical about the way they discoloured.

Combine that with the guitar's effortless playability, and this example certainly has us green with envy…

1963 FENDER STRATOCASTER

Fender was a rapidly expanding business in the early 1960s, and the Stratocaster underwent production changes throughout 1962 and again in 1963

For many players, the Strat reached its apex in the early 60s. The reputation of guitars from this era among players was such that when Fender's fortunes were waning in the early 80s, after buyers had become disillusioned with CBS-era Strats, a slab-'board 1962 model was selected as the basis for a new series of historically accurate reissues that helped turn the company's fortunes around.

By 1963, however, the Stratocaster had moved on again. In order to address production problems Leo Fender had experienced with slab-fretboard necks, he introduced round-laminate 'boards part-way through 1962, which entailed gluing a thin, curved layer of rosewood onto the top surface of a maple neck that had already been cut to the correct radius. It was a trickier piece of workmanship and marked a new phase in the guitar's development.

This battered but beautiful '63 Stratocaster in Fiesta Red is currently on show at the vintage Valhalla that is Guitars: The Museum in Umeå, Sweden. It's a long journey north, unless you currently reside at the Pole, but if you want to feast your eyes on this gorgeous slice of Strat history and more besides, you could do a lot worse than pay a visit.

SET TO STUN

S-1 switching features alongside the Shawbucker bridge 'bucker on this fully loaded Strat. Pickup expert Tim Shaw tells us more about his new design

Earlier in 2015, Fender announced the Shawbucker-equipped American Standard and American Deluxe guitars. While the guitars themselves are pretty standard Fender fare, the Shawbucker is lesser known. Its designer is Nashville-based Tim Shaw, who won't mind being classed as a veteran of the musical instrument industry, with spells at both Gibson and Fender – and, interestingly, it's Tim's spell at Gibson that informs this new pickup design. One of Tim's earliest teachers was pickup legend Bill Lawrence – "I learned a lot from him about pickups and circuits," says Tim, which sounds like understatement – but it was at Gibson's old Kalamazoo plant that Tim's research began in earnest.

"I got there in '78 and met Walt Fuller, just about the time he retired," continues Tim. Fuller was working on what was to become the Heritage 80 Les Pauls, and the job of the pickups fell to Tim. "I had a lot of information from Seth Lover; I had his mimeograph sheets with all the specs and vendors of the materials for the original humbucker."

For a variety of reasons, the materials had changed. "You see, magnets at that time... well, it wasn't a precise science, so the Alnico mix could change – that was one variable."

Then there was the coating of the copper coil wire, which had changed from the thicker and more expensive plain enamel to thinner and more cost-effective polyurethane (known as single poly with trade names such as Polysol).

"So, a coil wound with 5,000 turns of plain enamel-[coated] wire takes up a little more room than 5,000 turns of wire coated with single poly and it sounds a little airier because it's got lower capacitance," Tim explains. "This was a detail that no-one cared about at Gibson at the time – the new poly coating was cheaper and more consistent, so they changed. Then the magnet material changed from Alnico II to V around '71, though that's not a documented change – hey, it's a magnet, it works, who cares? So there were a bunch of changes – either actively, the wire, or passively, the magnet – that had changed. When I started looking at the old stuff, I

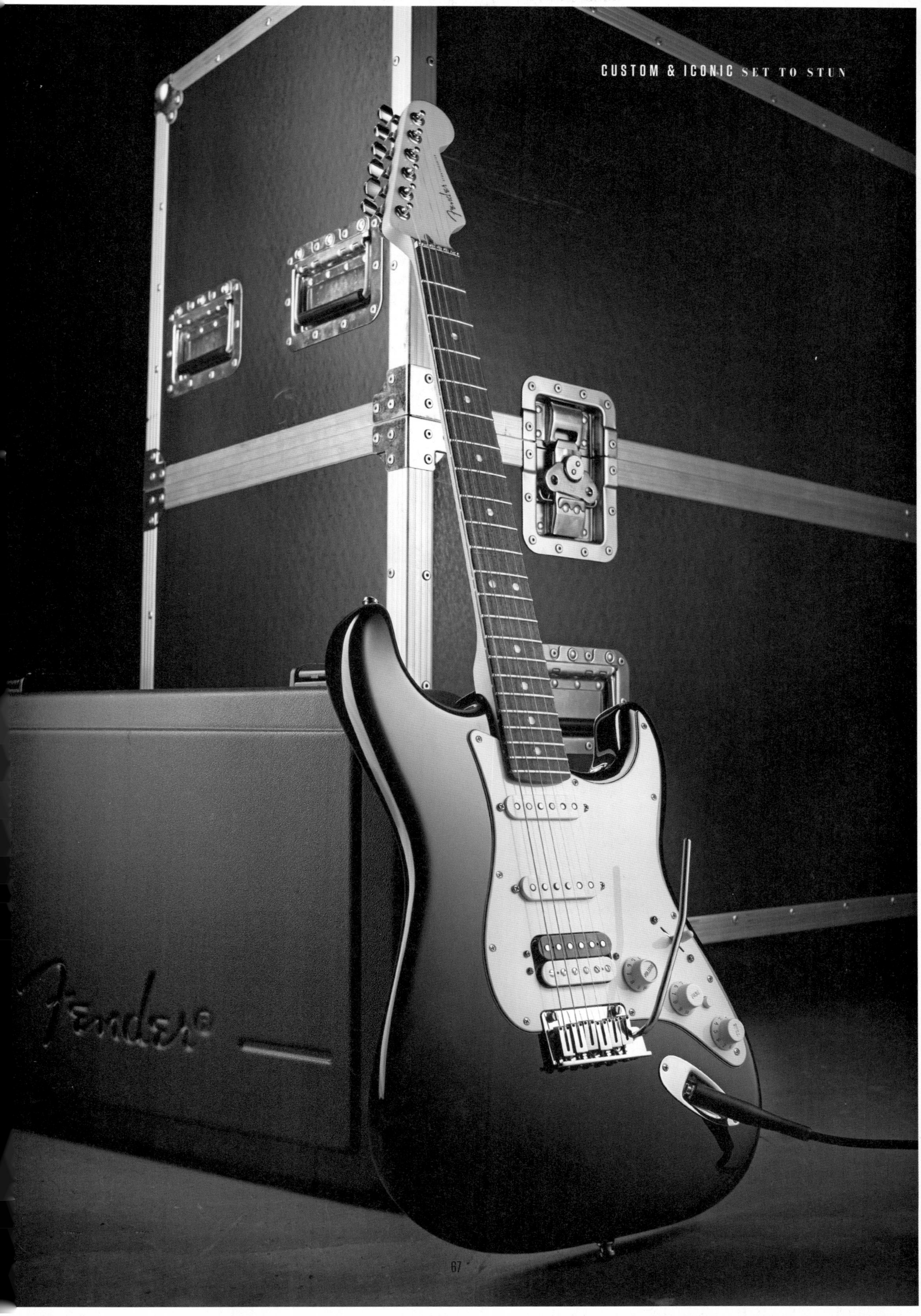
Fender

1

1. Alongside the new Shawbucker are a pair of 'noiseless' N3 stacked single-coil-sized humbuckers that use different Alnico magnets. If hum pick-up from standard single coils bothers you, these are extremely quiet

2. The tapered edge of the body heel requires a differently shaped neck plate. We also have Fender's Micro-Tilt neck adjustment, which makes setup far easier than a vintage-spec Stratocaster

3. More refinements can be found at the headstock with rear-locking tuners – which feature staggered-height string posts – and LSR's high-tech roller nut. These subtle tweaks dramatically improve the vibrato's return-to-pitch efficiency

realised whatever we were doing wasn't what we started out doing. And as people seemed to like these old ones, my charter was, 'Well, how close can we get?'"

The answer was pretty close indeed, and the 'Tim Shaw' humbuckers, made in Kalamazoo between 1980 and '84, are the stuff of legend.

Tim left Gibson in 1992, and was hired by Fender in 1996. It wasn't until he was asked to recreate his humbucker for Fender in 2013, however, that the Shawbucker project started. Tim and his research team built some prototypes to his original recipe.

"We had original spec and some hotter ones, overwinds of 42 gauge wire and stuff. We listened to them. Fender's Justin Norvell picked the one he liked, which was the one I liked, and it ended up in the Strat you have there. So Alnico II magnet, plain enamel-coated wire and it's not potted, not waxed at all. There is an airier quality, a kind of transparency that you get when you don't pot them. Also, it's pretty much the lowest output, with a DC resistance of around 7.6kohms: the lower end of the humbucking wind."

Aside from the zebra Shawbucker, things look pretty standard here. Modern Fender features such as the two-post vibrato, staggered-height locking tuners, LSR roller nut and a compound-radius fingerboard (plus a very slick setup) are present and correct, but the S-1 switch within the volume control knob and an additional push switch above the dual tone controls tell us this is no standard ride.

2

3

"There's a very journeyman feel to the whole instrument, especially when you find your 'core' sounds"

The five-way lever switch selects the bridge, bridge and middle, middle, middle and neck and neck pickups in parallel with the S-1 switch in its up (or off) position. Depress the switch and the combinations slightly change and are primarily in series, not parallel, with some additional trickery.

For example, in position 1 we have the bridge humbucker and the middle pickup in series, not parallel, while position 2 combines them in series with 'a special capacitor' on the bridge pickup. Position 3 selects all three pickups in a combined series/parallel linkage, position 4 links neck and middle in series with a special capacitor on the neck pickup and, finally, position 5 links neck and middle in series. That small push switch instantly selects the bridge humbucker, bypassing the volume and tone.

FEEL & SOUNDS

The refined nature of the Deluxe is reflected in its feel, with the modern, slender but not over-thin and quite full-shouldered 'C' profile of the neck, larger frets, the compound radius

'board, and the chamfered corner of the neck heel – not to mention the slinky in-tune vibrato system. While initially daunting, the expanded sounds give you many options both in cleaner classic Fender territory and beefier gained situations. The first surprise is how matched the 'bucker is with the N3s. It's a little thicker, wider and smoother sounding, and a little louder, but tonally, there's plenty of Fender-y high-end bite. While the bypass sound may be a little bright for some, voiced with the volume and tone in circuit, that crispy high end is slightly attenuated and it really sits well with the 'noiseless' N3s. These units certainly don't pick up as much hum as a standard single coil in solo selection – mixed, they're even quieter.

Push the S-1 switch down and, in series, the bridge/middle selection sounds bigger and wider than the sole humbucker. Position 2 is more hollowed, a great rootsy low-gain rhythm sound, and position 3 is wider and darker but still very Fender-y. The two neck/middle selections provide another flavour of Fender funk. There's not a bad sound to our ears anywhere, although the N3s do sound quite

4

FENDER AMERICAN
DELUXE STRAT HSS
SHAWBUCKER
PRICE: £1,339 (inc case)
ORIGIN: USA
BODY: Alder
NECK: Maple, Modern 'C' profile, bolt-on with
Micro-Tilt adjustment
SCALE LENGTH: 648mm (25.5")
NUT/WIDTH: LSR roller/42.8mm
FINGERBOARD: Rosewood, 241-356mm (9.5-14")
radius
FRETS: 22, medium jumbo
HARDWARE: Chrome-plated 2-Point Deluxe
vibrato with pop-in arm, Deluxe staggered cast/
sealed locking tuners vibrato, vintage-style
tuners with Fender logo
STRING SPACING, BRIDGE: 54mm
ELECTRICS: Fender Shawbucker (bridge),
Noiseless N3 single coil-sized humbucker
(middle, neck), 5-position lever pickup selector
switch, master volume (with S-1 switch), tone 1
(neck), tone 2 (middle and bridge)
WEIGHT (kg/lb): 3.47/7.6
OPTIONS: Maple fingerboard, Sunset Metallic
and 3-Color Sunburst cost £1,399
RANGE OPTIONS: Other American Deluxe Strats
are available from £1,159. See www.fender.com
LEFT-HANDERS: No
FINISHES: Black (as reviewed), Olympic Pearl,
Sunset Metallic, 3-Color Sunburst. Satin
urethane neck; gloss polyurethane body
Fender GBI
01342 331700
www.fendercustomshop.com

'modern' – bright-edged and hollowed, less
thick and chunky compared with Texas
Specials, for example – but that balance
between the humbucker and the N3s means
you're not contrasting balanced levels.

There's a very journeyman feel to the whole
instrument, especially when you find your
'core' sounds, whatever they might be. It's
obviously oh-so-Fender, but the Shawbucker
addition doesn't mean, like some, that we have
a Fender/Gibson duality. Sure, you could use it
like that, but to our ears, this is 100 per cent a
Fender guitar with a low-output clean, clear
humbucker that really works. Is it the 'best'
PAF-alike out there? Well, there's an open,
uncompressed voice here that really suits and it
might just change your view on humbucking-
pickup-equipped Strats. Frankly, our much
loved old Road Worn feels like a museum piece
in comparison.

VERDICT

If you prefer a more conventional drive, then
we'd suggest the cheaper Shawbucker-
equipped American Standard, but the raft of
upgrades on offer here – not to mention the S-1
switching – kicks the Deluxe into a different
league. It's more refined, and will suit someone
who knows their guitars and needs a lot of
sounds from a single instrument.

4. The new Shawbucker is
highly vintage-informed and
falls into the low-output side of
the PAF-alike humbucker. It's
very different from the high
power 'buckers that were a
common mod in the 80s

"It might just change
your view on
humbucking-pickup-
equipped Strats...
Our much loved old
Road Worn feels like a
museum piece
in comparison"

9/10

PROS A hugely refined Stratocaster with
low-output bridge humbucker and versatile S-1
switching

CONS Vintage purists, or indeed lovers of high
output 'rock' HSS Strats, should look away

RAGGED GLORY

It's 20 years since the Fender Custom Shop started bashing up its guitars so we didn't have to. We talk to Fender's Custom Shop director Mike Lewis about the latest pair of relic guitars to leave the workshop – the Ancho Poblano Strat and Tele Caballo Tono

Just how does Fender keep coming up with new spins on designs that originated over six decades ago? Well, the Ancho Poblano Strat, named after one of the most popular peppers grown in Mexico (called 'Ancho' when dried and 'Poblano' when fresh), started with a tone quest. "I wanted to create something that had a spicy flavour but not overly hot," says Mike Lewis, Custom Shop head, sounding like a celebrity chef.

"Sometimes hot pickups can cross the line in terms of tone, lack some highs and don't have that clear, classic Fender sound. So I wanted something that was a little bit hotter and I thought, 'What if we went progressively warmer from the neck to the bridge, then on the neck and the middle pickup we could somehow calibrate them for a string-to-string balance so the first two strings could be a little more accentuated?' Then on the bridge pickup we went to a completely different design from the other two with flat-pole magnets, which are Alnico V versus the Alnico III of the neck and middle, and we're using enamel wire on the bridge as opposed to Formvar wire on the neck and middle. The flat poles, magnet type and enamel wire creates a different sound, a little more aggressive.

"From there, the idea was simple: we've got big-sounding pickups, let's focus on big. Big is better: big neck, big sound; big frets, big sound – so let's do it."

The Caballo Tono comes from the Cabronita, which Mike says "was very well received. But here, we injected a little more Telecaster into it; it's got Cabronita DNA and some original Esquire prototype DNA, which is where the Cabronita evolved from. It's simple. Put a Tele pickup in there, keep the TV Jones, put on the Tele control plate and change the name to reflect what it is: a real tone horse!"

But the hardware is far from vintage. "The original Tele bridge has a certain sound quality that's hard to replicate – it's the whole thing... The RSD bridge retains all the things that make the Tele bridge sound the way it does. But the tray isn't as tall, so it's easier on your hand. The saddles are still brass so you get that sound, but you can intonate them better. It's a really good job; it was designed by Scott Buehl, one of the master builders."

JOURNEYMAN

The Custom Shop is known for its Time Machine guitars, or 'Relics' as they're called. These two have different treatments, all part of the imagined 'story' behind the guitar. "This year is the 20th Anniversary of the Relic and the original guitars were very much like the Journeyman – pretty lightly aged. Over the years, our customers have asked us to beat 'em up more, that's why we have the Heavy Relic and Extreme Relic, but the Journeyman takes us back to our roots and our standard Relic."

73

FENDER 60TH ANNIVERSARY STRATOCASTERS

To celebrate the Stratocaster's 60th birthday a few years ago, Fender brought us upgrades on three of its most popular and important variants. Did these upgrades breathe new life into an old classic?

The mind boggles when one realises that the Stratocaster is over 60 years old. We said the same on its 40th and 50th anniversaries, of course, but this guitar really could have come off the drawing board six days, let alone six decades, ago. Putting it into context, that same year, Dwight Eisenhower and Winston Churchill were both still in office.

At the bottom of our price ladder comes the Mexican-made 60th Anniversary Classic Player 50s Strat; in the middle sits the 60th Anniversary American Standard Commemorative Strat; and topping out this birthday trio is the 60th Anniversary American Reissue 1954 Strat. You'll forgive us for sticking to more manageable abbreviations throughout this review.

CLASSIC PLAYER 50S STRATOCASTER

There was little wrong with the Classic Player even before Fender gave it the 60th Anniversary treatment. With its great build quality, value and vibe, we loved the 9.5-inch radius 'board, medium-jumbo frets, American Vintage Strat pickups and tuneful two-post vibrato with stamped-steel saddles. In fact, it's hard to know how Fender could improve on such a winning formula, but improvements there are. These include an ash body, vintage-style locking tuners, gold anodised pickguard and backplate, commemorative neckplate and headstock medallion, gold hardware and gloss nitrocellulose finish.

That final detail should tell tone hounds that this Classic Player occupies a loftier space than its already illustrious predecessor. It comes in Desert Sand finish that gives off an ultra-cool 'surf' aura, with its gold anodised aluminium plate and tinted plastic parts.

Mexican build quality rarely disappoints. In fact, it's impossible to find a flaw of any kind throughout this guitar's construction or finish.

In the hand, the Classic Player's gently V-shaped neck is neither too thin nor too fat. Strung with 0.010-gauge strings, which actually feel lighter, the action was perfect for almost any style and one could noodle on it all day.

The Classic Player's two-point vibrato reduces friction: but not with the purists

AMERICAN STANDARD COMMEMORATIVE STRATOCASTER

Available in 2014 only, the American Standard Commemorative Strat is an impressive-looking animal. Dressed in classic two-tone urethane 'burst over a two-piece side-jointed ash body, it brims with special features.

Again boasting an anniversary commemorative neckplate and headstock medallion, here, the heel is dressed away at its corner for improved access. Further aiding playability is a compound-radius 'board carrying the Standard's usual 22 medium-jumbo frets. Other high-end touches include gold hardware, pearloid tuners and pearloid dot markers.

The American Standard usually features Fat 50s pickups, but here, Fender graces it with a trio of special-design 1954 single coils. They sit in a parchment pickguard with similar-coloured knobs and switch and the Standard's usual control set-up; these include the No-Load tone that acts on bridge and middle pickups. From zero to nine, it works normally, but turn it full up and it's bypassed for "increased output and overall tonal response". For our video demo, we kept it fully clockwise to take advantage of that extra zing.

The Standard's neck is a slim, slinky affair that's a little wider than its two siblings, and with its compound-radius fingerboard, feels even slicker. The satin finish is drag-free, and the fat frets and low action beg for speedy licks and big bends. Fender fits it with 0.009-gauge strings that feel rather floppy – we appreciate the guitar is perhaps aimed at younger players, but surely a pro instrument should come with 0.010s? That aside, it's classy and modern, and we can think of few Strats less 'standard'.

AMERICAN VINTAGE 1954 STRATOCASTER

And here's where it all started! Although looking like any other Two-Colour Sunburst, maple-necked Stratocaster, the 1954 differs in certain respects. The headstock edges are rounder, as are the pickup edges too; the polystyrene knobs and selector-switch tip are slightly stockier than on later versions of this model. Early Strats in general tended to have deeper body contours; Fender is spot-on with the '54, and it instantly feels 'right'. It looks great in flash-coated nitro lacquer, too.

The body is two-piece, side-jointed ash, but so expertly have the pieces been joined that it took us minutes to locate the faintest line running under the jack socket.

Pickups are newly designed 1954s, and Fender says they sing with the tone of the originals. These would have been mated to a master volume, two tones and a three-way switch; however, the more usable five-way is fitted and the former is supplied, should your vintage sensibilities win out.

Although possessing the fattest neck of the three, it's also incredibly comfortable, filling the palm and seeming effortless to play. In hindsight, Fender got it right with the 7.25-inch radius, as playing barre

chords doesn't tire the hands, and pushing string bends 'up the hill' makes real sense. Limited to a run of 1,954 units, the American Vintage 1954 looks set to become a collector's item. And that's a shame, because it cries out to be used and abused, gain dings and dents and become a patina-laden musical instrument – not a pristine museum piece!

SOUNDS

You can hear the three guitars demo'd in our videos. Each went through our house AC15 with the same settings and no outboard trickery, so any differences you hear belong to the guitars themselves.

Generally speaking, the Classic Player was darkest; its tones were fattest and most 'rounded'. It accepted overdrive beautifully, and thickened further as a result. There's no need to change these pickups: so no 'pimping' costs further down the line!

The middle-priced guitar was the brightest. And although we kept the No-Load tone control bypassed, this was still evident on the neck pickup, which is not affected by that pot. The light strings could be something to do with it, but whatever the reason, we liked this brightness as it stacked up beautifully in our track. It's the most versatile of the three, no question.

Sitting sonically in the middle of our trio is the American Vintage 54. If you know what a great Strat sounds like, then picture it in your mind, and this is it. Better still, check it out on the video demo.

VERDICT

So, three Strats, three price points – and three very different guitars on show. We're often asked: "Aren't they all the same?" and this trio gives the answer better than the most eloquent writer ever could. Fender has put thought into the balance of features, materials, hardware and electrics and come up with three superb guitars to float the boats of very different guitar players.

Priced and styled to capture hearts, the Classic Player is a peach. It looks wonderful, its vintage-meets-modern neck won't offend a soul, and its big, fat tones make it the blues-rocker's new best friend.

The American Standard Commemorative is the Strat fully formed for today: sonically, it's the most versatile, and its neck, frets, dressed-away heel and compound-radius 'board mark it out as the modern-player's guitar.

And so to the '54! What better accolade to Leo and Freddie's design – that the present company can remake it as closely as this, and still it sets pulses racing and fingers flying? It marked the art of the maverick genius back in 1954, and it marks the art of musical instrument production engineering today – albeit laced with real heart and soul.

60 years on, Fender should be congratulated for not only upholding the legacy of the world's most recognisable electric, but also for continuing to push the boundaries of quality and choice with these terrific guitars.

FENDER 60TH ANNIVERSARY CLASSIC PLAYER 50S STRAT

PRICE: £994 (including tweed plush-lined case)
ORIGIN: Mexico
TYPE: Double-cutaway solidbody electric
BODY: Ash
NECK: Tinted maple, with 6-a-side headstock
SCALE LENGTH: 648mm (25.5")
NUT/WIDTH: Synthetic bone/ 42mm (1.650")
FINGERBOARD: Integral maple with 241mm (9.5")
FRETS: 21, medium jumbo
HARDWARE: Gold anodised aluminium pickguard and back plate; commemorative neck plate and headstock medallion, 2-point vibrato with stamped-steel saddles, vintage-style locking tuners
STRING SPACING, BRIDGE: 53mm/2.08"
ELECTRICS: 3x Fender American Vintage single coils with volume and two tones (tone works on bridge pickup), 5-way switch
WEIGHT (kg/lb): 3.63/8
OPTIONS: None
RANGE OPTIONS: See 60th Anniversary American Vintage Strat
LEFT-HANDERS: No
FINISHES: Desert Sand (as reviewed)
Fender GBI
01342 331700
www.fender.com

GUITARIST RATING

	★★★★✩
Build quality	★★★★★
Playability	★★★★✩
Sound	★★★★✩
Value for money	★★★★★

Guitarist says: Almost impossible to criticise, the 60th Anniversary Classic Player 50s is a stunning Strat.

FENDER 60TH ANNIVERSARY AMERICAN STANDARD COMMEMORATIVE STRAT

PRICE: £1,498 (including tweed 60th Anniversary plush-lined case)
ORIGIN: USA
TYPE: Double-cutaway solidbody electric
BODY: 2-piece side-jointed ash
NECK: Maple, with 6-a-side headstock
SCALE LENGTH: 648mm (25.5")
NUT/WIDTH: Synthetic bone/42.8mm (1.685")
FINGERBOARD: Integral maple with compound-radius 241mm (9.5") to 355.6mm (14")
FRETS: 22, medium jumbo
HARDWARE: Gold. Commemorative neck plate and headstock medallion, 2-point synchronised vibrato with bent-steel saddles, pearloid button tuners
STRING SPACING, BRIDGE: 53mm/2.08"
ELECTRICS: 3x Fender special design 1954 single coils with volume and two tones (second No-Load tone pot works on bridge and middle pickups; full up bypasses tone control), 5-way selector switch
WEIGHT (kg/lb): 3.4/7.5
OPTIONS: None
RANGE OPTIONS: See 60th Anniversary American Vintage Strat
LEFT-HANDERS: No
FINISHES: 2-Colour Sunburst (as reviewed)

GUITARIST RATING

	★★★★✩
Build quality	★★★★✩
Playability	★★★★✩
Sound	★★★★✩
Value for money	★★★★✩

Guitarist says: The modern Strat for the modern player – the culmination of the breed, if you like.

FENDER 60TH ANNIVERSARY AMERICAN VINTAGE STRAT

PRICE: £2,278 (including tweed 60th Anniversary plush lined case)
ORIGIN: USA
TYPE: Double-cutaway solidbody electric
BODY: 2-piece side jointed ash
NECK: Maple, with 6-a-side 1954-style headstock
SCALE LENGTH: 648mm (25.5')
NUT/WIDTH: Bone/41.3mm (1.625")
FINGERBOARD: Integral maple with 184.1mm (7.25") radius
FRETS: 21, vintage narrow
HARDWARE: 'Nickel chrome' vintage vibrato with bent-steel 'Patent Pending' saddles, vintage-style tuners
STRING SPACING, BRIDGE: 53mm/2.08"
ELECTRICS: 3x Fender special design 1954 single coils with volume and two tones (tone works on bridge pickup), 5-way switch
WEIGHT (kg/lb): 3.63/8
OPTIONS: None
RANGE OPTIONS: There are six guitars in the 60th Anniversary range. As well as those reviewed, there's the Squier 60th Anniversary Classic Vibe 50s Strat (£478), the American Deluxe Stratocaster Plus HSS (£1,774) and the Deluxe Stratocaster HSS Plus Top with iOS Connectivity (£814)
LEFT-HANDERS: No
FINISHES: 2-Colour Sunburst (as reviewed)

GUITARIST RATING

	★★★★✩
Build quality	★★★★✩
Playability	★★★★✩
Sound	★★★★★
Value for money	★★★★✩

Guitarist says: This is where it all began – there wasn't much wrong with it then, plus it's even better-built now.

Buddy Holly And The Crickets
perform *Oh, Boy!* on the
Ed Sullivan Show in 1958

LEO'S MASTERPIECE

Over 60 years on, the world's most imitated and iconic electric guitar still satisfies the needs and fires the imaginations of players

Judged solely on the sheer variety of music that has been created with the Stratocaster in the past six decades, it would qualify as a classic. But its appeal is deeper than that – arguably, it's more sophisticated than the workmanlike Telecaster, but also simpler in control layout and functionality than the Jazzmaster that followed in 1958.

In other words, for many players,the Stratocaster is the 'Goldilocks' guitar of all Leo Fender's creations. Its blend of tonal versatility, playability and looks turned out to be 'just right' for thousands of players since 1954. In starting with a blank canvas, without decades of guitar-making heritage behind

him (or even personal knowledge of how to play a guitar), Leo Fender turned those potential handicaps into virtues – by beginning with the question: what do guitarists need from their instrument? Leo put the question to the leading players of the mid-50s, such as Western Swing guitarist Bill Carson, who suggested ways in which the Telecaster could, in his personal view, be improved, including a ribcage contour for comfort and extra pickups.

The value of a talented engineer asking that simple question of players can be judged by the fact that the Stratocaster is not simply still with us, but has inspired so many other cool variations on the solidbody, twin-cutaway guitar in the years that have passed since '54.

Guitarist

OFFICIAL APPAREL STORE

PREMIUM GARMENTS
FOR PICKERS

Guitarist
ESTABLISHED
1984

ONLY £20

Wear your passion for six-strings with pride, with our new line of Guitarist-branded premium cotton tees – available in a range of cool colours and classic designs

https://bit.ly/guitarist-merch

IF LEFT WAS RIGHT

Fender introduces a Hendrix-inspired guitar priced to appeal to younger fans, but which could inspire any guitarist lusting after that elusive 'cool' factor

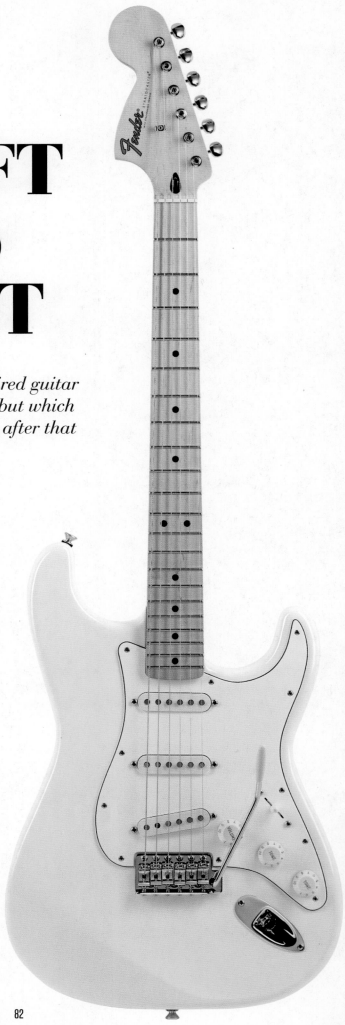

W hen we heard that another Hendrix tribute Strat was in the offing, the groans were audible. Often in the past, the great man's name has been used with less sensitivity than we would have liked. After all, he's not here to sanctify any of these products or decisions. The spec, too, seemed odd – a right-handed guitar with upside-down headstock and reverse-angled bridge pickup; surely it could only end up being the proverbial canine's supper?

But it's nothing of the sort. Built in Fender's Ensenada, Mexico factory, the Jimi Hendrix Stratocaster is available in Olympic White or Black, both with maple neck, tinted pickups and knobs on a white-black-white pickguard. Mexican Fenders are built supremely well; their polyester finish is exemplary and their necks never anything but great. Yes, this one's headstock is upside down and, yes, its bridge pickup is reversed, but these facets – the consequence of Jimi turning a regular Strat upside down – contributed greatly to its playability and sound in his hands.

For example, the longer bass string travel to the farthest tuners meant greater tension and better tuning stability when drop tuning, as Jimi did, and the consequently slacker treble strings meant smoother bends and vibrato. Also, the 'wrong way round' pickup served to

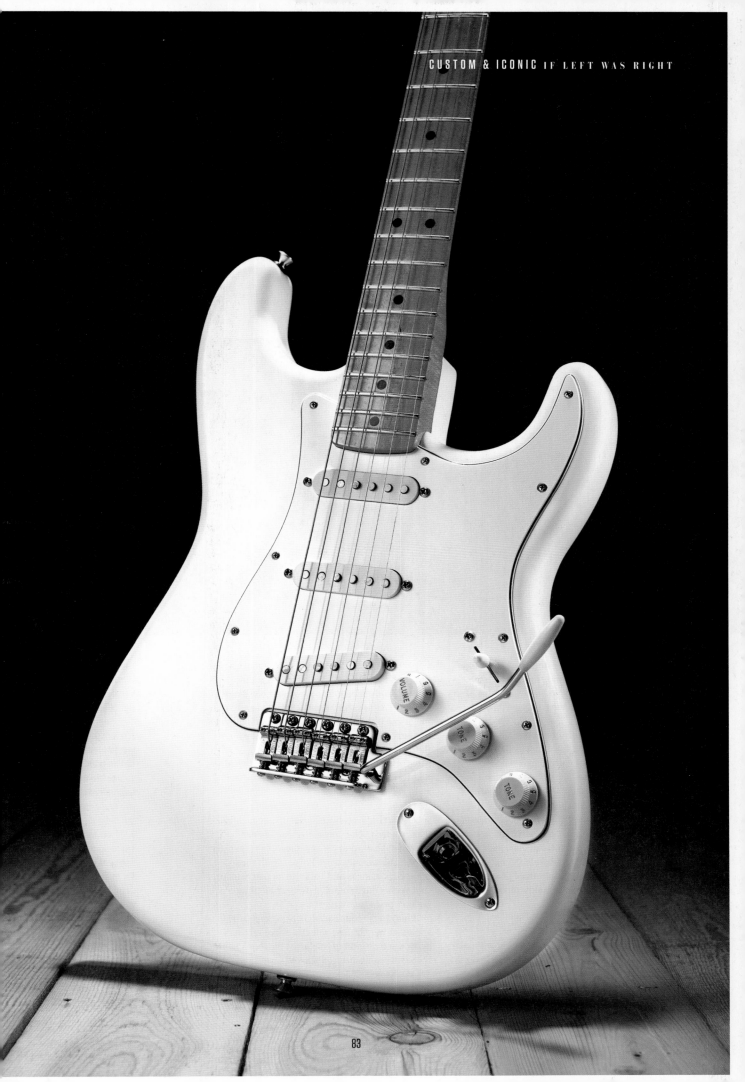

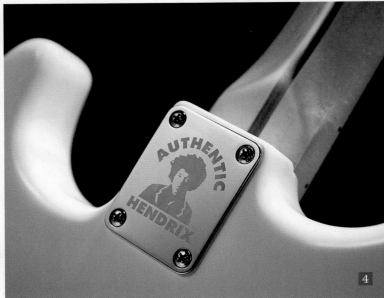

moderate the treble for a slightly thicker tone on the top strings and marginally more twang one on the lower ones. And actually none of this makes the guitar look weird, as we'd predicted it would.

Fender has sensibly chosen not to switch the vibrato block round (Jimi's upside-down Strat's arms protruded awkwardly from the top), while opting for modern-style headstock truss adjustment is a concession that makes sense.

Two elephants in the room, though: the smaller being that the body is right-handed and not upside down; the larger is that a tribute instrument to the greatest left-handed guitarist ever, is not available left-handed! The latter of these is surely due to economics but seems, well, strange; the former makes tons of sense, as we'll see.

FEEL & SOUNDS

Anyone who's watched Hendrix play will have noticed that his reversed Strat offered little upper-fret access. In fact, he didn't play up the dusty end much at all. Our guitar's right-handed body solves that problem in one fell swoop. The neck's shallow 'C' shape is mega-comfy in the hands and Fender's other modern twist – medium-jumbo frets on a flatter, 241mm (9.5-inch) radius 'board – adds greatly to the experience. Our guitar's action was too low to dig in like Jimi, with the top string almost choking off when going for big bends, but a quick adjustment of the first and second strings' bridge saddles and playability was restored. The vintage vibrato works well, coping with Jimi-style excesses and returning to pitch admirably. It's a joy to try all those great riffs, chords and solos on an instrument that seems much more grown-up than its meagre price tag suggests.

Plugging in, our Hendrix Strat instantly shows its mettle. The selector's five settings bring out a quintet of recognisable tones from these fine-sounding '65 USA Vintage

1. Available in white or black (Woodstock or Isle Of Wight!), the body and neck are perfectly finished in polyester

2. Tinted pickup covers and knobs contrast nicely with the white 'guard, while a vintage-style vibrato offers reasonable wobble and divebomb capability

3. The large, post-'65 Strat headstock looks cool when flipped over, especially with the 60s-style Fender logo the right way up. Some say the added mass even adds something to the tone, while the modern truss rod certainly makes adjustments easier

4. A four-bolt neck-plate proclaims 'Authentic Hendrix' to denote that this is an official release in conjunction with Jimi's estate. His image etched into the plate, and 'Jimi Hendrix' signature on the headstock, are registered trademarks

5. Angling the bridge pickup this way, with the treble end further from the saddles and the bass nearer, adds depth to the top strings and twang to the lower ones, and surprisingly, looks quite normal

5

Stratocaster pickups. All the sounds are bright, but not overly so, and the bridge pickup does seem somewhat tamed by its treble pole pieces' greater distance from the bridge. Favourite settings? Neck and middle, then middle (very *Hey Joe*); then neck (*Wind Cries Mary*). The bridge unit comes into its own when drive is applied – the more the merrier for those lairier 'voodoo' moments.

VERDICT

Despite initial reservations, we came to really like this guitar. It doesn't look odd at

"You barely notice the 'wrong way round' bridge pickup – which was the thing we feared might look the weirdest"

all – in fact, the upside-down post-'65 headstock with Fender facing the 'correct' way makes one feel almost anarchic playing it. What's more, you barely notice the 'wrong way round' bridge pickup – the thing we feared might look the weirdest. And if these changes to the basic Strat's formula do add a spark of Jimi magic to tone and playability, all the better, although it's hard to tell without a similarly equipped 'regular' Mexican Strat for comparison. That said, its range of tones from the USA pickups – a good move by Fender – is full of Strat-y personality, and that, and the use of the occasional Gibson aside, was the essence of the Hendrix tone.

Apart from needing a tiny action tweak, it was hard to fault this guitar in build, price or execution. In fact, more than one *Guitarist* 'old hand' has said how cool it would be to turn up to a gig with one. And if you can turn the heads of a bunch of old cynics like us, Fender is clearly doing something right!

FENDER JIMI HENDRIX STRATOCASTER
PRICE: £689 (inc gigbag)
ORIGIN: Mexico
TYPE: Double-cutaway solidbody electric
BODY: Alder
NECK: Maple with walnut skunk stripe and reverse headstock with Hendrix signature
SCALE LENGTH: 648mm (25.5")
NUT/WIDTH: Synthetic bone/42mm
FINGERBOARD: Maple, integrated with neck, 241mm (9.5") radius
FRETS: 21, medium-jumbo
HARDWARE: Chrome-plated vintage vibrato, Kluson-style six-a-side tuners
STRING SPACING, BRIDGE: 55mm
ELECTRICS: 3x Fender US Vintage 65 'grey bottom' single coils, 5-way lever pickup selector, master volume and 2x tone controls (neck and middle pickup)
WEIGHT (kg/lb): 3.59/7.9
OPTIONS: None
RANGE OPTIONS: Mexican Standard Strats start at £480, including left-handers
LEFT-HANDERS: See range options
FINISHES: Olympic White (as reviewed), Black

Fender GBI
01342 331700
www.fender.com

8/10

PROS Real Jimi vibe; plays and sounds great

CONS Not available left-handed

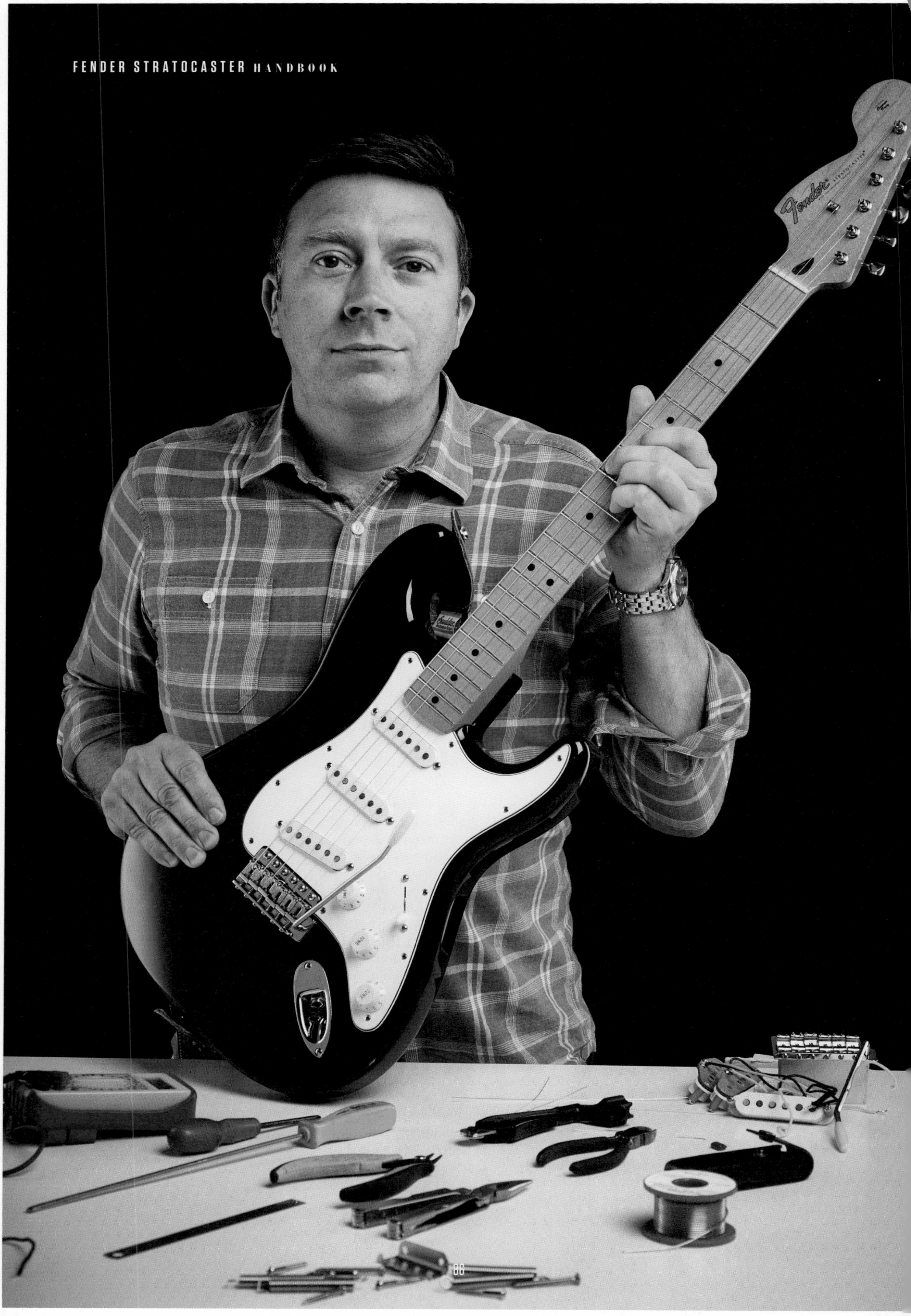

BRIDGING THE GAP

Tone Doctor Simon Law – tour tech to Robben Ford and numerous other guitar greats – takes a stock Mexican-made Fender Jimi Hendrix Strat and pimps its bridge and pickups to demonstrate how you can tweak an off-the-peg guitar to better prepare it for life on the road

When I told a guitar-playing friend that I was going to be writing an article on this guitar, he pointed out, "Hendrix sounded great on any guitar." Well, of course! But lest we forget, the guitars our heroes were playing in the 50s and 60s were the best of the best, particularly Jimi, who was rocking late-60s, big-headstock Strats. Still, with the right tools and guidance, we can get quite a bit extra out of this off-the-shelf Strat.

Our Mexican-made model features a right-handed body and an upside-down left-handed neck. Tonally, it's a little thin in timbre and not hugely resonant; the output is quite low and could be more assertive. Of course, much of this is down to the neck and body wood, but the hardware and, more importantly, the bridge can be changed to one of a higher quality that features a solid steel trem block. I will also be swapping out the pickups and tidying up the wiring...

Before we start, it's always a good idea to note some measurements. First, as we're going to be swapping the bridge, note down all the string heights. Using an accurate ruler, measure the distance between the strings and the top of the 12th fret [1] – it will normally be 1.5 to 2mm, depending on personal preference. Second, measure the distance between the strings and the top of the outside pole pieces of each pickup. The bridge pickups will normally be a little closer than the neck pickup.

GET TO WORK

Now, it's time to tear it apart! I mean, disassemble... All you need for this whole job is a pair of side cutters, a couple of small screwdrivers and a soldering iron [2]. Start by removing all the strings (let's treat the guitar to some nice new ones) and then remove all the small scratchplate screws from around the outside of the plate. Using a soft cloth, carefully turn the plate over to expose the beauty of the wiring... Uh oh: bird's nest! [3] This may be a nice-looking guitar with a fine black and shiny finish, but under the cover it could be tidier. Start by making some notes of where the three white wires from the pickups attach. They attach onto the switch in a particular order, meaning you get the right sound from the right click of the switch, so take a close-up shot with your camera phone. Using a 25- or 30-watt soldering iron, carefully desolder these wires from the switch along with the group of three black wires that make up the negative or ground on the back of the volume pot. Now, you can carefully remove the screws that hold the pickups to the scratchplate. The screws can normally stay in the plate along with the small rubber spacers or springs on the underside.

Carefully fit the pickup covers to your new pickups, making sure to use the right pickup in the right position – they should be marked B, M and N, for bridge, middle and neck. Roughly adjust them to a similar height to your previous ones. Once all three pickups are in place, we can get wiring. This is where we can have some fun – and make it look lovely and tidy, just the way Leo Fender would've liked it. Most vintage-style replacement pickups feature cloth-covered wire and this can be bent into nice right angles and cut to perfect lengths. Starting with the bridge hot/white wire, carefully lay the wire down along the pickup, across the volume pot and to the switch. When cut to length and soldered onto the switch, it should look immaculate, as if it had been done at the factory in the 1950s.

Next, you can move onto the middle pickup. Take the white wire towards the bridge pickup then bend it

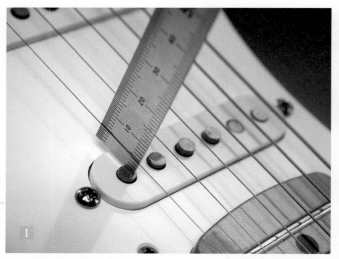

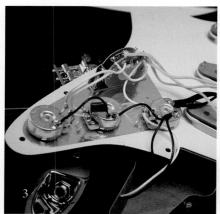

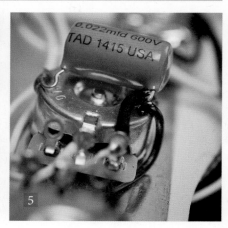

at right angles down across the bridge pickup and to the switch and solder. Repeat this for the neck pickup, each time taking great care to measure twice before cutting the wire to length. Now, we can group all the black wires together and solder them to the back of the volume pot, once again making sure you have them straight and looking perfect before trimming them to length and soldering. Gone is the pile of spaghetti, replaced with order and correctness! [4]

It's time to replace the okay-sounding and rather naff-looking tone capacitor with a lovely sexy-sounding orange one made by Sprague or Tube Amp Doctor (TAD) [5]. Of course, tone caps don't do a huge deal when you're not using the tone controls, but cheap ones will bleed too much tone and volume to ground once you do use them. Some Strats are wired so the tone control is out of the circuit when the bridge pickup is on its own. This, in my opinion, is the most useful time to have the tone control in the circuit, because you can reduce the unwanted and shrill high-end down a little by rolling the tone control from 10 down to eight – thus creating the singing lead Strat tone as used by such players as Jeff Beck, Eric Clapton, Matt Schofield and Eric Johnson.

This can be easily modified by identifying which wire goes from the switch to the back tone control. Then, using a small jumper wire, link the next unused tag on the switch to this wire, or just move this white wire along to the next lug on the switch, giving you a useful tone pot on the bridge pickup. It sounds tricky but, if you look at how the switch is working, you can see where the signal will be routed and work out how to route it differently. Such fun.

Finally, reassemble the scratchplate to the guitar with the tiny screws. You can test the function of the pickups without strings by very gently tapping the pole pieces of the pickups with any small non-magnetic screwdriver. Any faults should be easy to recognise and rectify at this point. Next, we can move onto the bridge.

YOUR NEW BRIDGE

In my opinion, steel is the only material that should be used for a vibrato block on your Fender Stratocaster. This has to be pure steel, not steel that has lead or zinc in it. Both of these alloys will kill sustain and dampen clarity. Many companies make replacement hardware for Fender style guitars; my favourite is Callaham from the US and this is what I will be using here.

First, remove the backplate (if fitted) and remove the springs that attach the trem block to the steel trem claw [6]. Do this very carefully with long nose pliers (andwatch they don't fly straight up towards

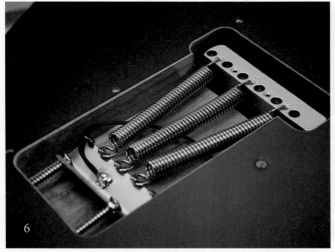

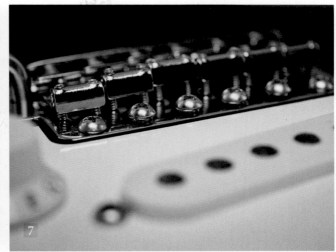

your eyes – I've done it and it isn't nice!). Next, remove the six screws that attach the trem to the top of the guitar. You should now be able to lift the old unit up and out of your guitar. Roughly match the bridge saddles of your new unit to the old one, in both height and back and forth (intonation). Now to fit the new unit...

Place it in the body rout and line up the six mounting holes. Roughly fit the screws so they're approximately 1mm from the top of the baseplate [7]. Flip the guitar over so you can fit the springs. Fit the hook end of the spring into the trem block and then, using a longer bladed flat screwdriver through the hole in the spring, let it slide down onto the trem claw... clonk! [8] This can take a few attempts and you may find it easier to use pliers, but it's hugely satisfying to do it this way. Hold the spring in block with one finger, screwdriver into spring hole. Put the screwdriver just behind the trem hook and let the spring slide down the shaft of the driver. Done. Repeat for the other springs.

Next, back to the trem mounting screws... I like to adjust the outer two screws of the six to be just touching the trem baseplate – and I mean just touching so as not to hinder the settlement of the bridge at all. I then set the centre four screws to be just above the baseplate by about 0.5mm. With this

adjustment, none of the screws are hindering the trem sustain at all.

Now, you can restring the guitar and make any adjustments to return the instrument to the starting specification, which, of course, should be a bit easier due to the better quality bridge unit [9]. I prefer the trem to be adjusted flat to the body, but with not so much tension on the springs that I can't just wobble a chord or note a little. Some players like a fully floating trem set so that a backward bend of the bar raises the note by a whole tone or even more.

Once you've tweaked, experimented with, and checked the intonation and you've adjusted the pickups for both output and balance from string to string, it's time to check out your guitar in all its new sonic glory. You should have a guitar with more power, sustain, clarity and overall quality of tone – certainly a guitar worth playing. Plus, the new pickups should improve both tone and touch sensitivity. In this feature I fitted some pickups made by the UK manufacturer Rog B pickups, but let your own ears and fingers be the judges. US makers such as Jerry Amalfitano, Lindy Fralin, Seymour Duncan and Ron Ellis – not to mention UK guys such as Mark Foley of Fat Boy Guitars and Tim Mills from Bare Knuckle – all make staggeringly great quality pickups for both Fender and Gibson guitars.

HEROES

HEROES

STRAT LEGENDS

When Leo Fender's masterpiece double-cut turned 60, we saluted and studied the techniques of the players who made the Stratocaster famous. From single-coil twang to Floyd-equipped shred, join us as we celebrate the guitar they said would never catch on…

BUDDY HOLLY

The leader of the Strat pack; the hero of our heroes

Buddy Holly was taken far too soon, at the age of just 22 in an air crash on 3 February, 1959, immortalised by Don Henley as "the day the music died" in his 1971 song *American Pie*. In that time, Buddy had created a rock 'n' roll blueprint of two guitars, bass and drums that would inspire McCartney, Lennon, Dylan, The Stones and many more.

He would do more to popularise the Stratocaster in the decade of its inception than any other artist. An accomplished guitarist, aside from his songwriting genius, Buddy brought a hybrid of rhythm and lead to fledgling rock 'n' roll at a time when single-note guitar breaks had been popularised by the likes of Scotty Moore. Though Fender had launched the Stratocaster three years previously, the appearance by Holly's band The Crickets playing *Peggy Sue* and *That'll Be The Day* on the Ed Sullivan Show on 1 December, 1957 thrust the guitar into the spotlight. Buddy Holly (born Charles Hard Holley) bought his Strat on 23 April, 1955 with money he loaned from his brother Larry, at Adair Music in Lubbock, Texas. He would own four more Strats (two of which were stolen while on tour) before his death.

Essential Strat Tone: *Peggy Sue*

"The Strat had never sounded more sleazy"

DICK DALE

The silver surfer with the red-hot riffs

In the early 60s, he'd been a pioneer of surf-guitar, and while souped-up Fender amps and reverb played a part, Dale insisted the Strat was the cornerstone of his brittle, tremolo-picked tone. "The sound is a Stratocaster guitar," he once noted. "It's the solidity of the wood. The thicker the wood, the bigger and purer the sound. It was a Strat. Not the Jaguar, not the Jazzmaster."

The surf scene wiped out, and Dale looked washed-up, but in 1994, he was at the heart of the most electrifying movie credits sequence of the age. "Any of you fucking pricks move and I'll execute every motherfucking last one of you!" screeches Honey Bunny at the start of Quentin Tarantino's *Pulp Fiction* – and so begins the warp-speed, staccato-note thrill-ride of Dale's *Misirlou*. The Strat had never sounded more sleazy, seedy or downright dangerous.

Essential Strat Tone: *Misirlou*

JIMI HENDRIX
Waving the Strat-spangled banner

James Marshall Hendrix is famous for many things – and he had a Strat slung around his shoulders for most of 'em. Left-handed guitars were even harder to come by in Jimi's 60s heyday, so he flipped his Strats over and restrung them back-to-front.

This approach helped to shape his tone – the slanted bridge pickup gave more treble to his lower strings and a darker tonality to the high strings, while his tendency to jam his guitar's three-way pickup selector in between pickups was partly responsible for Fender introducing the five-way pickup selector. Singling out Hendrix's Strat highlights is an unenviable task, but the graceful dexterity of *Little Wing* and outlandish aggression of *Voodoo Child (Slight Return)* are up there, for sheer control and tonal majesty alone. Yet it's impossible to ignore the iconic moments: the rendition of *The Star-Spangled Banner* at Woodstock, each time teeth met string, and *that* guitar-burning incident at Monterey. To quote Hendrix, "I decided to destroy my guitar at the end of a song as a sacrifice. You sacrifice things you love. I love my guitar."

Essential Strat Tone: *Little Wing*

FREE AUDIO FILES
FILESILO.CO.UK/
GBUK-033

Track 23

JIMI HENDRIX PARTIAL CHORDS

Jimi often used the 'in-between' pickup selection to augment his rhythm ideas. In typical Jimi style, our riff outlines a major chord by using lots of other related notes. It creates a rich weaving sound that's much more sophisticated than playing straight chords.

JIMI HENDRIX WAH/DIST LEAD

Track 24

Jimi would often use the middle pickup for both lead and rhythm, and a wah pedal is the icing on the cake. Our example showcases Jimi's minor pentatonic lead playing. Notice the C# and F# notes taken from outside **the E minor pentatonic scale to add colour.**

Val Wilmer/Redferns/Getty Images

BUDDY GUY

Knocking the spots off other bluesmen

When Guy hit the Chicago circuit in 1957, he was the wildest Strat cat in town, opening shows by bursting through the front doors playing guitar on a 100-foot lead, and ripping out feral solos that terrified his Chess Records paymasters. "I've been playing guitar with fire my whole life," he says.

Essential Strat Tone: *Justifyin'*

THE INBETWEENERS

From its launch in 1954, the Stratocaster was fitted with a three-way pickup selector switch, offering a choice of using each pickup on its own. Soon after, many players started to realise that by carefully positioning the switch between each setting, the Strat would produce two extra sounds. These 'in-between' settings would produce a thinner, quacky sound, and guitarists would often use matchsticks or toothpicks to hold the switch just-so.

It took 23 years, but in 1977 Fender finally resolved to fitting the five-way switch that is now standard, appeasing tonehounds, and putting a dent in the toothpick industry.

And, in case you are wondering, the position switches start at the bridge pickup (1) and follow up to the neck pickup (5).

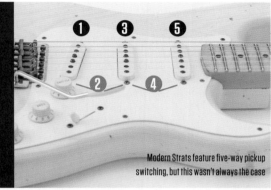

Modern Strats feature five-way pickup switching, but this wasn't always the case

Cliff's gift to Hank Marvin of a Fiesta Red Strat was a gift to modern British guitar music

© Keystone/Hulton Archive/Getty Images

HANK MARVIN

The British invasion

There were perks to being the sideman of teenybopper king Cliff Richard in 1959 – not least the chance to secure one of the first Strats on British soil. "Cliff wanted to buy me a good guitar, and we decided Fender was the way to go," recalls Marvin of his Fiesta Red model. "It came in a tweed case with red plush lining, and this magnificent-looking thing was just lying inside. It was like something from space, really, it was so futuristic in its design."

By 1960, Marvin secured his place in the Strat pantheon with The Shadows' hit instrumental *Apache*, which combined an economical twanged melody with expert wobbles of the revolutionary tremolo unit to create a vibe somewhere between surf-guitar and spaghetti western.

Essential Strat Tone: *Apache*

HANK MARVIN MELODIC LICK

Track 25

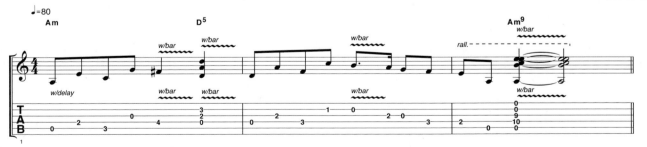

This example is in the style of early electric guitar pioneer Hank Marvin. Hank combined a glassy bridge pickup tone with subtle use of the vibrato bar, but picked the notes near the neck pickup to create his signature sound. Tape-style echo will bring things to life.

GEORGE HARRISON

Here comes the sun(burst)

February 1965 saw Beatles roadie Mal Evans purchase Strats at George Harrison and John Lennon's behest. Although Harrison recalled this as during the *Rubber Soul* sessions, The Beatles were recording *Help!* at the time, as proven by photos of Lennon at Abbey Road with one of the Sonic Blue pair Evans bought.

Nowhere Man is probably the most overt example of a Strat on a Beatles recording: George and John are playing their Fenders in unison. Harrison's Strat – neckplate dated December 1961 – would get a psychedelic makeover and become known as 'Rocky'. Post-Beatles, George chose a white Strat for the 1971 Concert For Bangladesh that some have speculated was assembled from the same haul of parts that yielded Eric Clapton's famous Blackie.

Essential Strat Tone: *Nowhere Man*

ERIC CLAPTON

Eric wasn't always a Strat man...

By the end of the 1960s, 24-year-old Eric was already a guitar hero, having played with The Yardbirds, John Mayall's Bluesbreakers and Cream. His guitars of choice had been Fender Jazzmasters and Telecasters, Gibson Les Pauls, ES-335s and SGs. However, once he unleashed the opening riff of *Layla* in 1970 – played on a 1956 sunburst Strat called 'Brownie' – Clapton and the Stratocaster were inextricably linked. 'Brownie' saw action during Eric's early 70s blues-rock heyday; his other celebrated Strat, 'Blackie', fashioned by Clapton out of three '56 and '57 model Strats, was his main guitar from 1973 until 1985. Since Eric's return to his blues roots in the late 80s, his Strat tones have come from Fender's EC signature models. The noiseless pickups and mid-boost circuit are the key to Eric's sound of the last 25 years.

Essential Strat Tone: *Cocaine*

CLAPTON'S 'WOMAN' TONE

Track 26

Eric began his love affair with the Strat in 1970 on the Layla And Other Assorted Love Songs album. His 'Woman' tone was originally performed on Gibson guitars with humbuckers, but you can replicate it by using a Strat neck pickup with the tone rolled off and the midrange on your amp **boosted**.

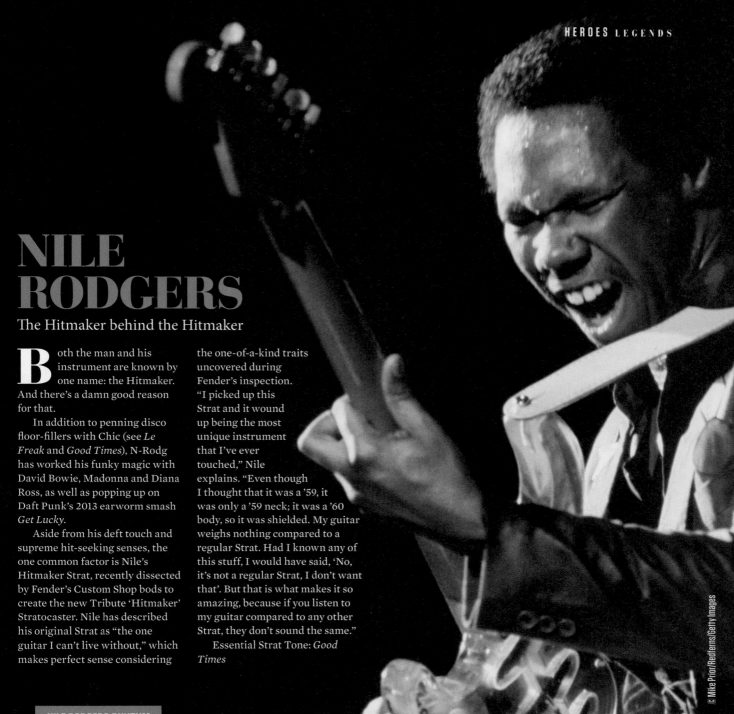

NILE RODGERS

The Hitmaker behind the Hitmaker

Both the man and his instrument are known by one name: the Hitmaker. And there's a damn good reason for that.

In addition to penning disco floor-fillers with Chic (see *Le Freak* and *Good Times*), N-Rodg has worked his funky magic with David Bowie, Madonna and Diana Ross, as well as popping up on Daft Punk's 2013 earworm smash *Get Lucky*.

Aside from his deft touch and supreme hit-seeking senses, the one common factor is Nile's Hitmaker Strat, recently dissected by Fender's Custom Shop bods to create the new Tribute 'Hitmaker' Stratocaster. Nile has described his original Strat as "the one guitar I can't live without," which makes perfect sense considering the one-of-a-kind traits uncovered during Fender's inspection. "I picked up this Strat and it wound up being the most unique instrument that I've ever touched," Nile explains. "Even though I thought that it was a '59, it was only a '59 neck; it was a '60 body, so it was shielded. My guitar weighs nothing compared to a regular Strat. Had I known any of this stuff, I would have said, 'No, it's not a regular Strat, I don't want that'. But that is what makes it so amazing, because if you listen to my guitar compared to any other Strat, they don't sound the same."

Essential Strat Tone: *Good Times*

© Mike Prior/Redferns/Getty Images

NILE RODGERS RHYTHM

Track 27

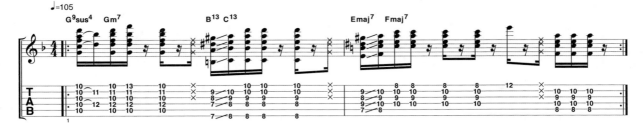

The amazing rhythm work of Chic's guitarist and producer Nile Rodgers is living proof that the Strat's neck pickup is great for funk. Use a relaxed, but well-timed, picking motion and target your pick over the neck pickup. A clean sound with stereo reverb will add some sparkle.

Weston-super-Mare's most famous son was a relatively late convert to the Strat

RITCHIE BLACKMORE

The pioneer of Neoclassical shred, inspired to pick up a Strat by Jimi

Weston-super-Mare's only bona fide guitar hero, Blackmore did marvellous things with a Strat while blazing a trail through Deep Purple and Rainbow. And that included smashing the beejesus out of them. Neoclassical shred, and the very existence of Yngwie Malmsteen in the guitar world, owe a heavy debt to Blackmore's hands, but his allegiance to the model that he's become synonymous with took a while. Up until *Child In Time*, from the classic 1970 Purple album *In Rock*, Blackmore had used his '61 ES-335 to cut every solo in the studio. But after he saw Hendrix live, he went on the Strat attack with the larger headstock 70s models – often literally: smashing them at the end of shows. But one of his favourites, the 1974 Sunburst model he used in one of his finest performances – in Munich with Rainbow in 1977 – at least lasted until 1980, when its headstock was broken off onstage.

Essential Strat Tone: *Black Knight*

"We stood there motionless, salivating"

JEFF BECK

Exploring parts that other Strat players can't reach

That can't be a standard Strat. Those can't be human hands. He cannot be of this earth. Such thoughts strike you when you see Jeff Beck in full flight. For Beck, the Strat isn't just a guitar, but a magic wand that has captivated him from childhood. "We stood there motionless, salivating, for at least five minutes," he recalls of his first schoolboy sighting in the window of Jennings Musical Instruments on Charing Cross Road. "We were freaked out."

Of course, every player on this list has dragged the Stratocaster into bold new territories. But when this pickless, peerless master achieves lift-off on his long-running signature model, the instrument has never sounded more like Heaven, as with a tickle of the whammy, a swell of the volume pot and a perfectly weighted bend, he creates an ethereal swoon like the orgasmic moan of a humpback whale.

Essential Strat Tone: *Where Were You*

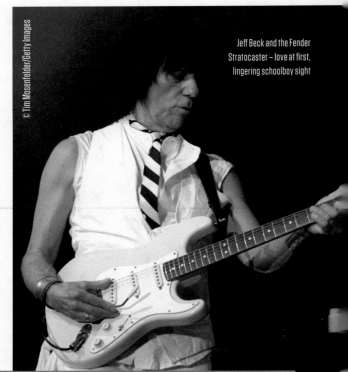

Jeff Beck and the Fender Stratocaster – love at first, lingering schoolboy sight

JEFF BECK SCOOPS AND DOOPS

Track 28

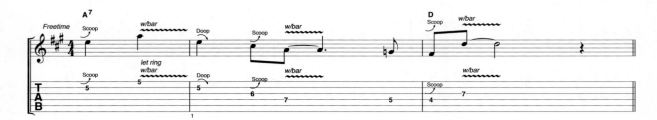

Beck got heavily into Strats in the early 70s. Our lick is perhaps more akin to his 80s style, employing fingerstyle and deft use of the whammy bar to 'scoop' in and 'doop' out of notes. Use a guitar with a two-point floating vibrato or a locking system to help with tuning.

Mystery surrounds the origins of David Gilmour's #001 Stratocaster

© Redferns/Getty Images

C-SHAPE

The all-rounder. Fender uses its C-shaped profile on many guitars, as it offers a familiar, medium depth and is comfortable for rhythm and lead playing. The modern C-shape offers a shallower, flatter profile, making it the perfect partner for a wider fretboard radius and big string bends.

U-SHAPE

This palm-filler is Fender's equivalent to the 'baseball bat'-style neck. It's thicker than a C-shape with a tighter curve, and Fender reckons it suits players who keep their thumb anchored in the back of the neck while playing.

V-SHAPE

The V-shape is perhaps the most divisive of the Big F's profiles. Its vintage vibe means that fans of 50s Strats swear by it. It creates a pronounced hump in your palm (that's what she said), allowing your thumb to comfortably fret notes over the top.

DAVID GILMOUR

The number one Strat fan

A man known not just for what he does with his Strats, but the stories behind them, too. Especially the pièce de résistance of his guitar collection: the #0001 Stratocaster. Understandably with a number like that, there's great interest surrounding the guitar's origins – though it is unlikely to be the first production Strat. It could have been a special presentation model made for an employee when they left Fender. Gilmour purchased the guitar from his long-time tech Phil Taylor in around 1977, though it took some understandable arm-twisting. "Eventually, Phil wanted to borrow some money to buy a house, so I blackmailed him!"

David explained. "I said the only way I'd lend him the money to buy the house, was if he sold me the white Strat..."

Guitarist's David Mead examined the guitar in 1986 and suggested it could well be a genuine 1954 model, and it's great that it's still being played by the man himself, rather than a museum piece. Just like Gilmour's far more modded mainstay, late 60s 'Black Strat' (neck now replaced) and his 1983 '57 red reissue. "There's something in the thinness and particular range a Strat has that makes it a Strat," he says of their unique appeal. Leo would be proud.

Essential Strat Tone: *Comfortably Numb*

GILMOUR CLEAN LEAD

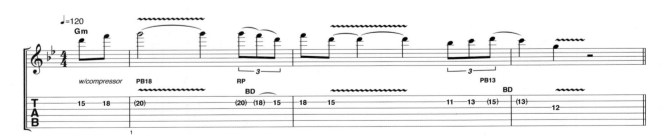

David Gilmour is famous for coaxing silky tones from his black 70s maple-necked Strat. We've used a compressor to bring out the sustain, particularly on the string bends. Add a long delay or a big reverb for authenticity.

STEVIE RAY VAUGHAN
A Strat, a Stetson and soul

The Strat is sometimes cast as the pedestrian choice of the ageing blues superstar. Tell that to SRV. Coming up on the hard-as-nails Texan circuit, the man in the Stetson went to war on his models, stringing them with heavy 0.013-0.058s and attacking bends and vibrato with such ferocity that he often had to pause sets to superglue the splits in his fingernails. "I like a lot of different kinds of guitars," he notes, "but for what I do, it seems a Stratocaster is the most versatile. I can pretty much get any sound out of it."

By 1983, *Texas Flood* had made SRV a star, and for the remainder of his career, he would rely on two much-loved models that crowds craned their necks for. The '65, known as Lenny, has the sweetest story, named in honour of SRV's wife after she blagged the funds to secure it for him. But for gearheads, it's the Number One hybrid that's the real treasure, comprising a '62 body, '61 V-neck, '59 pickups and left-handed tremolo.

Tragically, SRV himself never became an ageing blues superstar – he was killed in a helicopter crash in 1990 – but his soul-in-fingers Strat work still inspires and his Fender signature model continues to shift. Hats off.

Essential Strat Tone: *Pride And Joy*

SRV LEAD LICK

Track 30

SRV was fond of the neck pickup sound, and this lick is reminiscent of the way he sometimes navigated a turnaround section. We've employed a typical SRV trick of introducing the odd chromatic note (such as F and Bb in bar 1), which adds colour to a minor pentatonic lick.

ROBERT CRAY

Persuasive Strat tones

Robert Cray unusually opts to have his Strats fitted with hardtail bridges for stability

While the rest of the world got busy butchering their Strats with humbuckers and Floyd Roses, Robert Cray lead the charge for clean, bluesy Stratocaster sounds in the 80s. His funky rhythm style and smooth leads on hits such as *Right Next Door, Still Around* and *Smoking Gun* from his breakthrough album *Strong Persuader* cemented his place in blues history. He currently has two 60s-inspired signature Fender Strats, both with hardtails. Chorus pedal is not included.

Essential Strat Tone: *Because Of Me*

BONNIE RAITT

The queen of bottleneck

She bought it for "$120 at three in the morning in 1969", and Raitt's hybrid 'Brownie' Strat has been key to her weeping slide magic at every show since. Testament to her talent is that she's the first woman to be offered a signature Strat – even if she initially sent Fender packing ("I don't really want to hawk products").

Essential Strat Tone: *Gnawin' On It*

> "even if I was playing air guitar it would be with a strat!"

Yngwie's Strats have been mercifully obscuring the front of his trousers for decades…

YNGWIE MALMSTEEN

The forceful Strat virtuoso

The neoclassical shred merchant is as synonymous with the Strat as he is groin-grabbing leather trousers. It was 1984's *Rising Force* that brought Yngwie and his 1972 'The Duck' Strat to the forefront of shred-dom, owing to his Paganini-influenced playing and supreme harmonic minor chops. The speedy fretwork was partly down to The Duck's scalloped fretboard, which came about after a chance encounter with a 17th century lute:

"I was 12 or 13 years old, and I was apprenticing in a luthier shop. I saw a lute that had a scalloped neck, and I was fascinated," Yngwie recalls. "I took a cheapo, piece-of-crap guitar – one of those things you buy from a catalogue – and I made my first scalloped-neck model. It came out great."

Nowadays, Yngwie is more likely to be found wielding one of his signature Fender axes, but there's still only one model for him. "There's nothing else. A Strat is the guitar for me," he enthuses. "Even if I was playing air guitar, it would be with a Strat!"

Essential Strat Tone: *Rising Force*

TREMOLO (OR, HOW LEO GOT IT WRONG)

Despite not playing the guitar himself, it took Leo Fender just under half a decade to design two all-time classic guitars. Which is why we'll forgive him for creating the biggest misnomer in guitar history at the same time. The incorrect use of the word 'tremolo' was applied to the Strat's vibrato unit – an array of springs and metal based on technology Leo borrowed from his kitchen scales. Originally expecting it to be used for creating shimmering Hawaiian guitar, Leo mistook volume fluctuations (tremolo) for fluttering pitch changes (vibrato). The principle is simple; the bridge pivots on a fulcrum, balanced by the tension of the strings and retaining springs in the back of the guitar. When you depress the bar, you drop the pitch and the springs help to guide them back to their original pitch as you release the pressure. We're sticklers for giving it its true technical name in these pages, but even we'll admit – 'trem' sounds cooler than 'vib'.

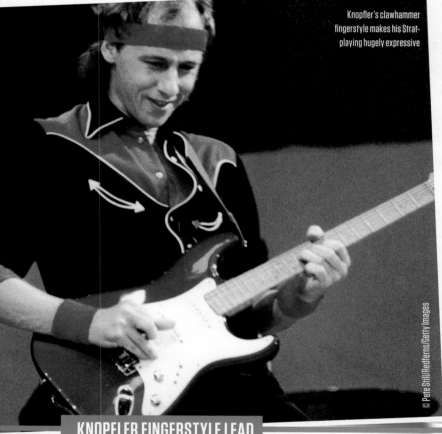

Knopfler's clawhammer fingerstyle makes his Strat-playing hugely expressive

(C) Pete Still/Redferns/Getty Images

MARK KNOPFLER
The sultan of strings

Through his playing with Dire Straits, solo material and soundtrack work, the Knopf has made his own mark on the world of guitar – and though he's wielded the odd Tele and Les Paul over the years, it's the Strat with which he made his name on rock staples *Sultans Of Swing, So Far Away* and *Walk Of Life*. Hank Marvin was the inspiration behind Mark's own red Strat – and luckily for us, Knopfler got hold of his '61 just in time to record the Straits' debut album in 1978. Part of what makes Mark's Strat sound so distinctive is his fingerstyle approach to the instrument, as well as his heavy use of volume pedals to further control his dynamics. It all adds up to a hugely expressive approach to phrasing, further emphasised by the Strat's trademark glassy tone.

Essential Strat Tone: *Sultans Of Swing*

KNOPFLER FINGERSTYLE LEAD

Track 35

This lick is reminiscent of Mark Knopfler's lead work on many early Dire Straits tracks. The most authentic results will come from using a fingerstyle approach, as Mark does. Mark generally picks with his thumb on every eighth note in licks such as this.

DAVE MURRAY

Maid-on a Strat

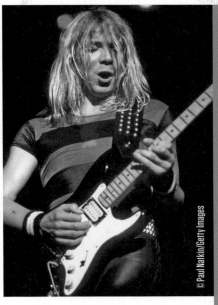

The Iron Maiden mainstay's most famous Strat, that he used on the band's first five albums, was actually owned by a guitar hero before him; the '57 was late Free legend Paul Kossoff's (you can see it when it was white on an old *Top Of The Pops* performance of *My Brother Jake*), and Dave Murray purchased it in 1976 after it had been refinished in black. He later had a pair of DiMarzio Super Distortions retrofitted.

Essential Strat Tone: *Run To The Hills*

(C) Paul Natkin/Getty Images

THE EDGE

Where the Strats have no name

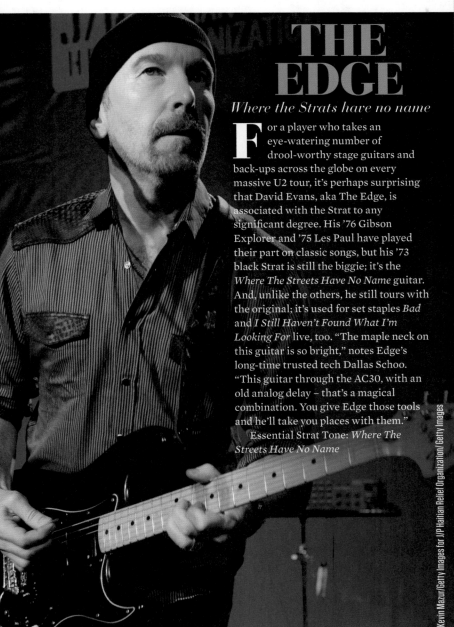

For a player who takes an eye-watering number of drool-worthy stage guitars and back-ups across the globe on every massive U2 tour, it's perhaps surprising that David Evans, aka The Edge, is associated with the Strat to any significant degree. His '76 Gibson Explorer and '75 Les Paul have played their part on classic songs, but his '73 black Strat is still the biggie; it's the *Where The Streets Have No Name* guitar. And, unlike the others, he still tours with the original; it's used for set staples *Bad* and *I Still Haven't Found What I'm Looking For* live, too. "The maple neck on this guitar is so bright," notes Edge's long-time trusted tech Dallas Schoo. "This guitar through the AC30, with an old analog delay – that's a magical combination. You give Edge those tools and he'll take you places with them."

Essential Strat Tone: *Where The Streets Have No Name*

(C) Kevin Mazur/Getty Images for J/P Haitian Relief Organization/Getty Images

TIME AT THE BAR... CREATIVE WHAMMY BAR TECHNIQUES

The Strat may not have been the first guitar to come equipped with a vibrato arm (Bigsbys were available in the 40s), but it is arguably the most iconic. Although some Strat players prefer their bridge 'decked' (set flat against the body), we recommend getting your vibrato system set up with a little movement so you can try out a few creative whammy bar techniques.

Track 31

1 DIVEBOMB AND REVERSE DIVEBOMB

To perform a divebomb, simply play a chord and dip the bar so the strings go slack, giving an explosion-like sound effect. A reverse divebomb means starting from slack and gradually raising the bar to give a sense of growing and getting bigger.

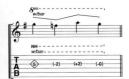

Track 32

2 WHAMMY BAR MELODY

Here, we've used the vibrato to play a melody. Our Strat's setup allows us to pull the bar upwards to raise the pitch by a tone, but this isn't necessarily the limit. On *The Attitude Song*, Steve Vai plays a two-tone shift using a Floyd Rose vibrato.

Track 33

3 SCOOPING INTO CHORDS

This is an atmospheric idea that uses the vibrato to 'scoop' into a chord. Simply dip the bar a touch as you strum. Make the most of the technique by raking your pick across the strings and adding gentle bar vibrato as the chord rings out.

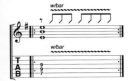

Track 34

4 RHYTHMIC PULSING

This is a textural rhythm effect, played by gently tapping either the bridge or the bar itself. For our example, we've played a straight eighth-note pulse on a chord, but you could experiment with your own different rhythmic ideas.

JOHN FRUSCIANTE

He can't stop playing Strats…

During his tenure as Red Hot Chili Peppers axeman, Frusciante became a contemporary Strat icon thanks to a rich vocabulary of Hendrix-inspired chordal embellishments and fiery solos. But while John's first contributions can be heard on 1989's *Mother's Milk*, it wasn't until *Blood Sugar Sex Magik* that his signature clean, compressed lines made their mark, most notably on riffy funkathon *Give It Away* and addiction ballad *Under The Bridge*.

Although funk was no longer the Chilis' primary concern following Frusciante's return in 1998, there are still plenty of stand-out Strat moments later on in the band's career, from *Scar Tissue*'s sparse hybrid-picked intro to the snappy riffs of *Can't Stop* and the Jimi-channelling solo in *Dani California* – John's recent solo work, such as 2009's *The Empyrean*, has its fair share of psychedelic Strat attacks, too. Frusciante is famed for his collection of endlessly desirable guitars, but none more so than his 'casters – John's favourite is an original '62 Sunburst, but he also owns '55 Sunburst and '61 Fiesta Red models, fitted with Seymour Duncan SSL-1 pickups. We're not jealous, honest.

Essential Strat Tone: *Under The Bridge*

FRUSCIANTE FUNK/ROCK RIFF

Track 36

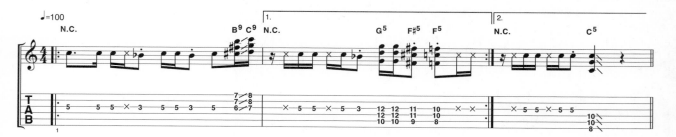

Former Chili Peppers funk-rock master John Frusciante is often pictured playing a beaten-up old Sunburst 60s Strat. Our example is a funky little ditty, reminiscent of some of his earlier work with the band. A clean, punchy Fender amp tone will bring the lick to life.

TOM MORELLO

Killswitching in the name

Although most famous for his Arm The Homeless mongrel axe, Morello also rocked the hell out of his 'Soul Power' Strat during Audioslave's incredible seven-year career. A stock FSR Strat, modified with a Floyd Rose and killswitch, the Soul Power fuelled a wealth of 'slave riff-fests, including monster singles *Cochise*, *Like A Stone* and *Your Time Has Come*.

Essential Strat Tone: *Cochise*

BILLY CORGAN

The infinite Strat-ness

The 90s saw a new slew of guitar heroes emerge from the US, but only one was loyal to the Strat. "It was never a choice of, like, yeah, I want to play a Stratocaster," Corgan said in an interview with Fender. "I just got one, and when I played it, it suddenly brought alive what I was looking for in music." The versatility of Corgan's back catalogue is a testament to the Strat's own adaptability, and in 2008 he was awarded his own signature guitar, modelled after his first Strat – a 1973 model.

Essential Strat Tone: *Cherub Rock*

© Ilan Dickson/Redferns/Getty Images

JOHN MAYER

In your Strat-mosphere

With chops evoking the spirit of Hendrix and SRV and boutique tone to match, John Mayer is a true modern guitar hero, and he achieved it all with the help of the Fender Stratocaster.

John has a large collection of Strats, including his Sunburst SRV signature model, the iconic battered 'Black 1', and a host of Jimi-inspired guitars.

"I have a prototype 1979 Hendrix Tribute Strat: white with a reverse headstock, with a contour on the front, and a prototype Hendrix Monterey Strat that [artist] Pamelina painted in 1997. I love prototypes! I have a '68 Strat, black, big headstock, classic Band Of Gypsys, and I have a '69 Olympic White Strat with maple cap neck, which is the Woodstock Strat."

The John Mayer Stratocaster has some unique features – string trees placed towards the end of the headstock to allow for more leverage when bending behind the nut, a thick C-shaped neck, and perhaps most crucially, John's 'Big Dipper' pickups. These have a scooped midrange, further accenting John's Fender-ish tone

Essential Strat Tone: *Vultures*

John Mayer's had even more drool-worthy Strats than he's had A-list romances…

JOHN MAYER LICK

Track 37

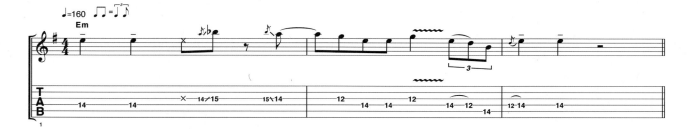

John Mayer is an exciting Strat player from the SRV school, so the neck pickup is featured regularly in his playing. This lick is all about hitting the strings hard with your pick and making sure your string muting is good. Dial in a clean sound with plenty of headroom.

KENNY WAYNE SHEPHERD

The spirit of '61

One of the key bluesmen of the post-SRV period, Kenny Wayne is a Strat man through and through, like his idol. A prodigious talent, he found his holy grail guitar at the age of 16 when he and his father visited Los Angeles and spied the '61 Sunburst Strat he fell for. Kenny returned a year later to buy it and it's barely left his side.

Essential Strat Tone: *King's Highway*

ALEX TURNER

Pluck it and see

"We're Arctic Monkeys... Don't believe the hype." These are the words Alex Turner spoke in the live video for *I Bet You Look Good On The Dancefloor*. Within weeks, Turner, his band and his fittingly Arctic White Standard Strat had rocketed to the top of the charts, clocking up the fastest-selling debut album in UK history. Often preferring 50s-style maple necks using the bridge pickup, Alex and his Strat tones have reinvigorated the spiky sound of indie-rock guitars, incorporating punk, 50s-inspired twang and surf, even drop-tuned riffing. These days, Alex tends to flit between Fender Broncos, Les Pauls and various Gretches, but it all started with the Strat!

Essential Strat Tone: *Fake Tales Of San Francisco*

SIMON NEIL

The Captain of modern Strat-rockers

If it felt as if the Tele had been lording it over its younger brother in the 2000s, that's probably because the Strat seemed to have fallen out of favour with modern indie bands. Except, that is, one of the biggest British breakthroughs of the last 20 years. Biffy Clyro's Simon Neil even goes as far as reviving Hank Marvin's Fiesta Red finish on his Strats, which create the massive tones that have made Biffy such a live force. "You need a big loud guitar sound to make a Strat sound full and heavy," he says, "as it's naturally very bright and undistorted, bright and jangly. I run it through my pedals of doom and try to make it sound like a volcano erupting! I love the shape of a Strat, too, I feel so comfortable with it." Fittingly, Simon was awarded with his own Squier signature model in 2010. "My very first guitar was a Squier, so it's come full circle," he tells us.

Essential Strat Tone: *Get Fucked Stud*

Simon Neil uses an array of pedals to make his Strat sound absolutely massive

SIMON NEIL'S DROP-TUNED ANGULAR RIFFING

TRACK 38

Simon Neil has used his Strat to produce Biffy Clyro's signature aggressive down-tuned riffing style. There's an angular feel to our riff, thanks to onbeat rests and offbeat notes, so timing is crucial. One-finger powerchords are a key part of the Biffy sound.

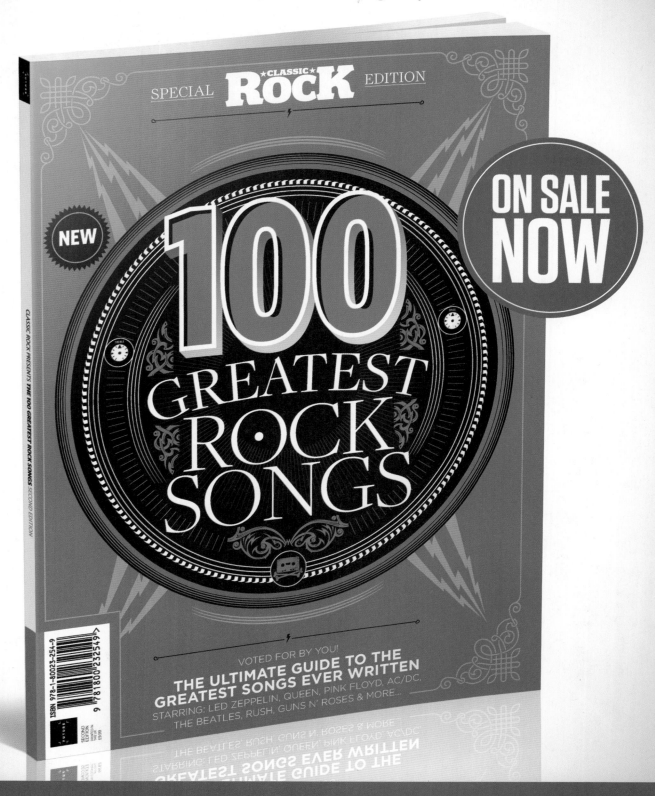

STRATO-MASTER

As The Shadows' King Of Twang, Hank Marvin was Britain's first guitar hero of the electric era, inspiring a generation of players with single-coil tones as springy and lush as a manicured lawn – but he also played the first Fender Stratocaster to reach these shores. We join Hank to hear previously unrevealed details of the Strats that he used to carve out his inimitable sound…

Few Strat play ers are as iconic as Hank Marvin – it's hard to picture him without also seeing in your mind's eye a Fiesta Red Strat with a maple fingerboard and gold-plated fittings, the guitar with which he made his name in The Shadows. It's a guitar that seemed electrifyingly modern in drab, post-war Britain, and in fact, it was the first example of Leo Fender's contoured masterpiece to enter the country. It's testament to the Strat's adaptability that Hank's still relying on the design decades later – and over the years, several other Strats have passed through the hands of this hugely influential player. As Hank prepares to cut a new album, we caught up with him to chat about the 'significant other' Strats that he's used on landmark recordings over the years, plus detailed insights into the Strat setup and component mods that he favours…

SO, THAT FIRST FIESTA RED STRAT. HOW DID YOU COME BY IT?

"That first Strat made an appearance in 1959. My Antoria had a horribly bent neck, so Cliff wanted to buy me a good guitar, and we decided that the Fender was the way to go, because we'd seen Buddy Holly with one on the Crickets album cover, and it was pretty cool. It was great looking, and we liked the sound of it, and we'd heard that James Burton used a Fender, so we got a catalogue from the States. We could see that Buddy's guitar was the Stratocaster and as that was their top-of-the-range model,

we assumed that James Burton would also have one. For some reason, we always thought it was called Flamingo Pink. But apparently they never had any such colour; it was Fiesta Red – anyway, we ordered that in what was pretty much the top-of-the-range specification."

ITS ARRIVAL MUST HAVE BEEN EXCITING?

"Very! It came in a tweed Fender case with the red plush lining and this magnificent-looking thing was just lying inside. It was like something from space, really, it was so futuristic in its design. The three pickups, the white scratchplate, the red guitar, the beautiful birdseye maple neck and all the gold plating, it just looked sensational. We just looked at it for a while, then took it out of the case, tuned it up and played it. Unfortunately, the strings were really heavy; I was told back in the 70s that they were sent out then with 0.013 to 0.056 gauge or something like that, with a 0.026 wound third, so they were much heavier than I was used to. I found it difficult to adjust to the effort."

SO DID YOU HAVE TO ADAPT YOUR STYLE OF PLAYING AS A RESULT?

"Undoubtedly – but the tremolo arm was great, because I found it helped me in different ways. The second string you could bend but probably only half a step, but I could bend it up with my left hand and pull it up a bit more with the whammy bar. The other thing was I could get vibrato on the strings, which I've always

Cliff Richard and The Shadows pose with their instruments c.1987

enjoyed in other instruments, to make it sort of say more. I could hit a note and dip it down or hit it under pitch and let it come up, just little things – and, of course, I loved giving it a good old shake. You know that trick where you push the second string up against the first and give the bar this wild shake, like the beginning of *Man Of Mystery*? Things like that were fun to do, and they were different. So, clearly, the guitar itself and the fact that it had the vibrato bar helped me to develop a style that wouldn't have happened without that.   Also, the guitar itself, the sound, the shape of it with the contoured body was very comfortable, and it's not a heavy instrument. So therefore you could swing it around a little bit for posing and leaping about. It lent itself very much to the visual aspect of rock 'n' roll."

SO WHAT WAS THE FIRST RECORDING SESSION YOU USED IT ON?

"I'm not sure about that. *Saturday Dance* [from August 1959 – Ed] has the Strat on it, and I used it on Cliff's second album [*Cliff Sings*]. We did things like *The Snake And The Bookworm*, but I don't remember which came first, that album or *Travellin' Light*."

IS IT TRUE THAT THE VIBRATO ARM WAS PARTICULARLY SHORT?

"Well, I didn't have anything initially to compare it with, but I noticed that some of the Strats I had later seemed to have longer arms. So I would say that it was shorter. It would be interesting to compare photographs."

THAT PARTICULAR GUITAR WENT BACK TO CLIFF, AND HE HAD IT

"You could swing it around a bit for posing and leaping about. It lent itself to the visual aspect of rock 'n' roll"

SPRAYED WHITE FOR A WHILE?

"Yeah, well, when Jennings [Vox's manufacturers – Ed] became the importers of Fender equipment once the trade embargo was lifted, they wanted us to use Fenders. Initially, I still had that first guitar, so Bruce [Welch] and Jet [Harris] got the Jazzmaster and Precision Bass. Then they said we could have red Strats and a bass, and we thought great, that would be a good look. They gave me one as well with a rosewood fingerboard, so the original went back to Cliff. That would have been 1961, and I think we had them sprayed white for a while. I know we had white Burns guitars, but before that, we had white Fenders during the time that Licorice [Brian Locking] was playing bass. We didn't have the red ones as well, so I think they took them back and sprayed them for us. Cliff liked the look of them, so he said: 'I'll get this one sprayed white, so when we're working together and I use it, it'll look really cool'."

WHAT WERE THE FIRST RECORDINGS THE ROSEWOOD STRAT WAS ON?

"The first session? That's a good question, but I can't remember! When we did the *Crackerjack* TV show playing *The Frightened City* and *FBI* [in late April 1961] we had those guitars, but we

At Wembley Stadium in 1989

A promo shot of The Shadows in 1961

didn't necessarily record and release things immediately. It could have been two weeks later, or a track could have been sitting around for months."

SO WHICH DID YOU PREFER AT THE TIME, THE MAPLE-NECK STRAT OR THE ROSEWOOD 'BOARD?

"I preferred the maple neck; it was a better guitar, I thought, with a particularly good sound. When I got the rosewood 'board, it just sounded a bit different to me. And I just preferred the feel of that original guitar, which was a particularly nice instrument with a nice fingerboard."

DID YOU GET A CHOICE OF THE GUITARS THAT JENNINGS SUPPLIED?

"No, they would just send them over. We just thought a Strat's a Strat, and if there was a problem they would obviously fix it – you know, rough frets or anything like that – but we didn't get to choose them ourselves; they picked out two guitars and a bass for us. There were at least two, maybe three sets going through from then until 1963. They replaced them as necessary. We did get newer guitars as ours got a bit bashed or whatever, and they'd take those back and do whatever they do with them, probably renovated and sold them, I guess."

AS YOU PREFERRED THE FEEL, WHY DIDN'T YOU GO BACK TO AN ALL-MAPLE NECK?

"Well, I asked, and they said they couldn't get the maple necks. Whether Fender had stopped making them at that point I've really no idea, but that's the story we were told and accepted."

HOW MUCH OF A PROBLEM WAS NOISE IN THE EARLY DAYS?

"It depended on the venue, particularly when they used the dimmers on the lights, as that seemed to affect the noise tremendously – it was really 'frying tonight'. Once you were all playing, it wasn't really that noticeable, but back then, people's sound-quality expectations weren't what they are now."

SO ARE YOU STILL FAVOURING KINMAN PICKUPS ON THE STRATOCASTERS THAT YOU USE TODAY?

"When we did the remake of all the old numbers for the Cliff and The Shads reunion album, I decided to try out some of the Fender '57 reissues, which I was introduced to when trying out the TVS3 echo. I thought it might be an idea to go back to the kind of pickups on the older guitars to get the sort of sound that we were trying to recreate. I had those fitted on all the guitars for the album, and they're still on! They sound really good. They have a nice twang to them, and although they're not as quiet as the Kinmans, they're not as bad as they used to be."

WHY DID YOU DECIDE TO SWITCH BACK TO FENDER GUITARS FROM BURNS INSTRUMENTS AFTER MARVIN, WELCH & FARRAR REVERTED TO BEING THE SHADOWS?

"Well, Iww'd already gone back to Fenders by then. When Marvin, Welch & Farrar were doing the Palladium with Cliff and Olivia Newton John, I had several guitars stolen – two Burns, a 12-string Gibson and an acoustic six-string – on the night before we opened. Bruce had lent Cliff's [now white] Strat to Terry Britten, who was in Cliff's band at the time, so he got it back for

Hank being filmed for *The Young Ones* and using his rosewood 'board Strat

Bruce Welch (right) holds the notorious humbucking Strat from the 1970s

Bruce Welch (right) holds the notorious humbucking Strat from the 1970s

me. I used it for the time we were there, then I decided, yeah I love it, I'm back on to the Strat! So that's when I bought the Sunburst one, or one with that terrible colour that looked like an undercoat, but anyway, I bought a Strat. I should have kept hold of Cliff's one!"

DURING THE TIME THAT YOU WERE WORKING WITH JOHN FARRAR, THERE WAS A SUNBURST STRAT WITH A MAPLE 'BOARD AND LARGE HEADSTOCK AND A MUCH-MODIFIED WHITE ONE...

"I had a black one! But, from memory, I had that sprayed at least once so that was probably the Sunburst one that I decided to have black, eventually with a tortoiseshell pickguard. I tried different pickups, too. I had a Fender humbucker on the bridge and something else on the front, a Gibson humbucker, I think, and a single coil. Actually, I still have that scratchplate in the studio with the pickups attached. I saw a black Telecaster in a guitar store in Manchester, and thought it looked really sharp, so I decided to do it black, and I had it for a few years until I gave it to Ben Marvin."

DO YOU HAVE ANY WIRING MODS DONE TO YOUR STRATS?

"Well, a few extra switches in the days when you tried to get those in-between pickups sounds, but I think that was on the one with the humbuckers. On one of my signature models, I've got a pull/push switch on the lower tone-control knob which does something, although I'm not sure what, as I've never used it! I think it engages the neck and bridge pickup together, and I think that's why I had it done. That's quite an interesting

sound, and I'm pretty sure I used that on a couple of my early album tracks, although it doesn't figure very highly on my Richter Scale of pickup choices – but you've just reminded me that maybe I should look at that again. I do use that between-pickups sound sometimes, just for a tone colour change, but usually, I use the pickups individually – and more often than not, I end up on the bridge pickup."

DO YOU STILL HAVE EASY-MUTE VIBRATO ARMS ON YOUR STRATS?

"Yes, I do, along with the block that Ian St John White does that matches the actual bar. The material it's made of stops the bar working loose like the standard arm tends to do. We've all tried tape and loads of things to stop that rattle, but these never do that, they're brilliant."

LET'S BE HONEST, THERE WASN'T ACTUALLY MUCH WRONG WITH THE ORIGINAL 1954 DESIGN, WAS THERE?

"No, not at all! I've seen a '54 belonging to a friend of mine in France, Jean-Pierre Danel, who's got one that he calls Miss Daisy, and it's very nice. Whew! Great design – looked great, comfortable to play... they got it right first time!"

IT'S TOTALLY FUNCTIONAL, BEAUTIFUL AND ICONIC AT THE SAME TIME...

"Absolutely! And it's a very practical instrument, too. They're as tough as old nails and you've got a variety of sounds available. I've seen people playing jazz on them; you can play country on them, blues, rock, heavy rock and everything you can think of, really. I think it's an incredibly versatile guitar."

LOVE TO PLAY GUITAR?

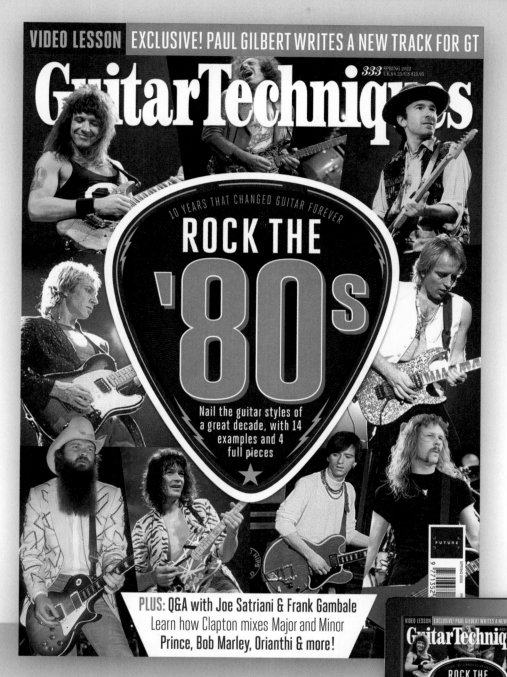

Then get properly serious with the world's finest tuition-only magazine. Every issue's packed with blues, rock, jazz, classical and folk lessons from the very best tutors, all with audio and backing tracks.

Print, digital and print/digital bundle offers at www.magazinesdirect.com

WE'LL MAKE YOU A BETTER PLAYER!

Guitar Techniques with moving tab synched to quality audio is available for iOS and Android

THE GUITAR MASTERY OF JIMI HENDRIX

It goes without saying that Jimi Hendrix is one of the most important guitar players in history – but he's also one of the most influential. In addition to the groundbreaking genius of his music, his playing style has inspired scores of guitarists of every genre since, many of whom have achieved legend status in their own right – think of Edward Van Halen, Joe Satriani, Kirk Hammett, Ritchie Blackmore to name just a few

We have already taken a close look at Fender's first affordable Hendrix signature guitar (see p82), but now we go deep into Jimi's playing style and show you some of the key elements of his playing that you can use to improve your own technique, as generations of guitarists have done from every corner of the electric guitar's broad church. So deep is Hendrix's influence on modern guitar playing, you may already use some of these techniques without even knowing, but such is Jimi's genius, there's probably a few you don't, too – his style really does contain something for everyone. We're kicking off with a look at Jimi's rhythm playing and his 'thumb over the neck' fretting technique, which forms the basis for most of his technique. Turn the page to get the Jimi Hendrix experience and don't forget to try these techniques out on your own Strat!

JIMI'S CLEAN RHYTHM STYLE

It all starts here! Get to grips with the basics of Jimi's 'thumb over the neck' and one-finger barre techniques and soon you'll be playing classic tracks such as 'Hey Joe', 'Bold As Love' and more

THUMB OVER THE NECK BARRE CHORDS

Track 15

G   Gadd9   G6   Gsus4

Classical guitarists may balk, but Jimi's 'thumb over the neck' barre chord technique allows him to position his fret hand in a way that those magical chord embellishments fall neatly under his fingers. It's just a matter of wrapping your thumb round the neck to fret the sixth string instead of using your first finger to barre across all six strings. Try the basic G chord first, and hammer on to the extra notes for a *Little Wing* or *Castles Made Of Sand* vibe.

FIRST FINGER BARRE CHORD SHAPE

Track 16

C/G   C/E   Am   Cadd9/G

This first-finger barre across three strings is a key part of Jimi's rhythm style. You *cannot* play like Hendrix without this shape. We've only scratched the surface but experiment with your second and fourth fingers, too. Start with the one-finger barre and hammer on to the additional notes in C/E, Am and Cadd9/G for authentic sounds in the style of *Bold As Love* and more.

MINOR CHORD SHAPES

Track 17

The 'thumb over the neck' and one-finger barre techniques also apply to minor chords. Remember, Jimi would often play only two or three notes from each shape – an idea that allows you to ditch the occasional note you can't easily reach and focus on cleanly fretting the more colourful extensions.

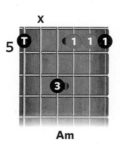

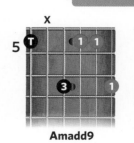

Am   Am7   Amadd9

TRIPLET HAMMER-ON PULL-OFF TRICK

FREE AUDIO FILES
FILESILO.CO.UK/
GBUK-033

Track 18

With a selection of Jimi's favourite chord shapes under our belts, here we look at one of his signature phrasing tricks that influenced players including Pearl Jam's Mike McCready and former Red Hot Chili Peppers guitarist, John Frusciante. The idea is to play a rapid hammer-on and pull-off to an extended chord tone (sus4 or add9, for example) using a triplet rhythm. Triplets are marked in notation with a '3'.

INSTANT HENDRIX CHORD PROGRESSION

Tracks 19-20

You might think there's nothing overly Hendrix-like in a G-Am-C-G sequence, but Jimi's rhythm work turns this basic progression into quite the signature line. The first two chords in our example, G (G-B-D) and Am (A-C-E), don't share any notes but in bar 1 we've added A, E then C embellishments. It's a trick on the ear that hints at both chords – and Jimi did this all the time. In bars 2 and 3 we're implying both Am and C chords throughout – you can even play these bars in the 'wrong' order. The bass guitar pins it all down with root notes to keep you on track.

MAJOR PENTATONIC PASSING BASS

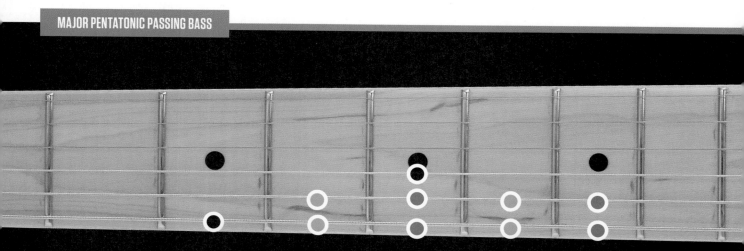

You've learnt our G-Am-C-G progression, now it's time to try another of Jimi's methods of navigating a chord sequence, this time with passing bass notes, *Hey Joe* or *Manic Depression* style. Black dots are G root notes, the red dots are from the G major pentatonic scale (G A B D E), and the green dots are 'chromatic' notes from outside the key signature. Simply strum one of the chords from the progression then experiment with the single notes to 'walk' melodically to the next chord.

JIMI'S FUNK-ROCK

He's arguably best known for his fiery, psychedelic lead guitar style but Jimi played with so much groove, too. TG looks at the more aggressively rhythmic side of the founding father of funk-rock

FUNK CHORDS

Get your fingers round these hard, edgy sounding chords and you'll be part way to nailing Jimi's aggressive funk-rock stylings. The 7#9 is the great man's best-known signature chord and can be heard in *Purple Haze*, *Foxey Lady*, *Crosstown Traffic* and more.

B7   B9   E7#9   F#m7

"The 7#9 is the great man's best-known signature chord"

SINGLE-NOTE RIFFS

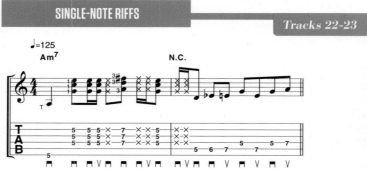

Some of Jimi's funkiest material was played with Band Of Gypsys. With a mixture of partial chords, fret-hand mutes and single-note pentatonic lines, this tab example will help you master the vibe of tracks such as *We Gotta Live Together*.

PLAY LOOSE AND TIGHT

Jimi could play tight or loose and this riff is an example of both methods, mixing up a *Foxey Lady*-style groove with the more strummy chords of songs like *Can You See Me*. Maintain a steady 16th note picking motion, relax into the C#7 barre chord and stay tighter on the F#7.

Just another day busting out the Hendrix moves

Work Experience: Jimi cut his teeth playing soul with Curtis Knight

JIMI'S SOUL STYLE

Before the pyrotechnics and psychedelia of The Jimi Hendrix Experience made him a household name, Jimi played on Nashville's Chitlin' soul circuit. Learn the guitar secrets of this lesser known side of Hendrix...

ASCENDING CHORD RUNS

Tracks 26-27

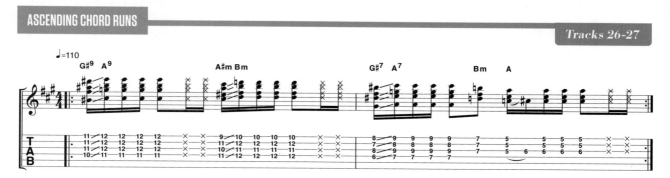

Jimi's soul, R&B and funk influences can be clearly heard in songs such as *Dolly Dagger*. This vamp, although based essentially on A7 and Bm chords, shows you how Jimi used inversions and other chord embellishments for a more varied and exciting vibe while keeping a tight and tidy soul groove.

119

MAJOR PENTATONIC SOUL RIFFS

Tracks 28-29

Here in this Curtis Knight-inspired example funky rhythms and single-note lines that spell out chord progressions are the order of the day. At the heart of our riff is a B7 chord but the fretting pattern resembles an open position G7 shape so keep this in mind as you play through the tab.

6TH INTERVAL SHAPES

Tracks 30-31

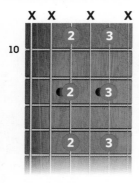

Major 6ths

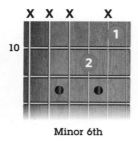

Minor 6th

These 6th interval diads are staple shapes in soul music and can be heard played by Jimi in a slightly rockier way on *Night Bird Flying*. These are two-note shapes so make sure you're able to play them with any pair of fingers (first and second; second and third; etc). We've used all four of the diads shown here in our audio example. See if you can work out which order we played them in.

CLASSIC BLUES LEAD

Tracks 32-33

Citing influences such as Albert King, Elmore James and BB King, it's obvious that Jimi was a disciple of the blues. This example borrows from such classics as *Red House* and *Purple Haze*, and also calls up *Don't Accuse Me* from Jimi's soul period. As was typical of his earlier work, we're switching between funky chords and bluesy minor pentatonic lead. Play the quarter-tone bends (marked with an arrow and a '1/4' in the tab) gently, but quickly, so they don't ring for too long – quarter-tones can sound lame if you hold on too long.

JIMI'S LEAD TECHNIQUES

Jimi's fiery lead guitar style revolutionised rock, influencing players as diverse as Stevie Ray Vaughan, Joe Satriani, Eddie Van Halen, John Frusciante, Kirk Hammett and more. We look at the techniques that broke the mould

STRING BENDS GET YOUR FINGERS ROUND THE MOST EXPRESSIVE OF LEAD TECHNIQUES

UNISON BENDS — Track 34

STACCATO BEND — Track 35

CATCH BEND — Track 36

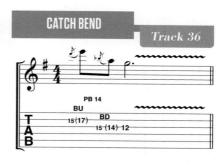

Check out the solos in *All Along The Watchtower* and you'll hear Jimi's unison' bends (two notes of the same pitch played at the same time – one with a string bend and one with a fretted note). You can play quickly and precisely, so you don't hear much of the bend up, or you can draw out the bend creating dissonance on the way.

Jimi loved this technique and used it in so many songs, perhaps most notably *Foxey Lady*. As you reach the peak of the bend touch the string with your pick to mute the note and create the staccato effect. Follow up on the next note with rapid BB King-style vibrato, rotating your wrist rather than moving just your fretting finger.

This tricky technique is a Jimi trademark made up of two string bends: a standard bend followed by a pre-bend on an adjacent string, which is then released. Simply roll your second finger across from the second string to 'catch' the third. The course of the first bend should automatically push the third string into a bend.

Get your various bending techniques sharpened up to capture Jimi's mojo

Hendrix's wah use was both creative and hugely expressive

WAH TECHNIQUE GET YOUR GROOVE ON WITH THIS THREE-STAGE LOOK AT JIMI'S WAH STYLE

VOODOO CHILD WAH — Tracks 37-38

CRYING BABY EFFECT — Tracks 39-40

FOLLOWING NOTES WAH — Tracks 41-42

The wah movement here keeps time on the quarter-note pulse, as if you were tapping your foot in time. The trick is to develop independence in your foot, so it doesn't follow the other rhythms you play with your hands.

The faster eighth note wah rhythm can be done on anything but tends to work best on single notes. This way you'll really hear the classic 'crying baby' effect that helped so-name the original Dunlop pedal. The faster wah action makes this much easier to play when standing up.

This vocal-like effect is great on cleaner sounds, where you can follow individual targeted notes rather than just moving in a constant rhythm. This is much more difficult and harder on the foot and ankle, so you might like to try this at a slower tempo initially.

HYBRID TECHNIQUES SOME OF JIMI'S MOST EXTREME SOUNDS CAME FROM MIXING DIFFERENT TECHNIQUES TOGETHER

PENTATONIC TRILL AND DIVE

TRACK 43

Simply depress your whammy bar while performing a trill with hammer-ons and pull-offs at the 12th and 15th frets on the second string to achieve this interesting ambulance siren-style doppler effect. For more extreme sounds, try it on the third string, which has lower tension.

"Jimi was so ahead of the times with his legato technique. His style spawned the fluid technique of many players"

LEGATO AND SLIDES

Track 44

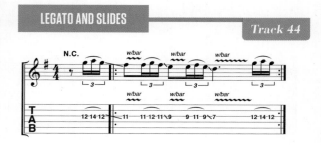

Jimi was so ahead of the times with his legato technique. His style spawned the fluid technique of many players including Richie Blackmore and Joe Satriani (and many modern shredders too) with this very idea. It allows for fast movement and coverage of the neck.

SLIDES AND DRONE

Track 45

Jimi's psychedelic and Indian influences can be heard in ideas such as this. The low E is used as a constant drone in the background while the octaves spell out notes from the E Dorian scale (E F# G A B C# D).

RHYTHM/LEAD CROSSOVER

Tracks 46-47

This example combines *Foxey Lady*-style chord playing with more technical fast pentatonic ideas in 14th position. Use all the available pull-offs to aid the speed of the final lick. You may wish to bend up and down in one motion in the final bar.

WHAMMY BAR TECHNIQUES JIMI PIONEERED THE AGGRESSIVE USE OF THE WHAMMY BAR AND INFLUENCED GENERATIONS OF SHREDDERS

DIVEBOMB TRILL

Track 48

This is one of Jimi's more extreme techniques and follows on from the pentatonic trill idea. It works particularly well on the fourth and third strings, but you should experiment all over the fretboard. Simply trill with hammer-ons and pull-offs between the 12th fret and the open note on your chosen string as you dip the whammy bar.

CLASSIC JIMI DIVE

Track 49

Unlike EVH's single-note divebombs with Van Halen, Jimi tended to favour using several strings for a more wild and out of tune sound that's not far off a demented car engine. Slide your hand up the fretboard then apply a divebomb in one continuous, fluid motion.

HARMONIC SCOOPS

Track 50

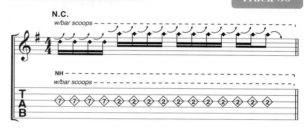

Jimi often used harmonics to coax feedback from his amp. If you're not playing at Jimi's ear-splitting levels use the higher harmonics at the 2nd fret to achieve a more biting effect. You can almost hear the influence on Dimebag Darrell's playing style. Make sure to dial in plenty of gain.

PLAYING BY FEEL SPEED UP OR SLOW DOWN – IT'S UP TO YOU AS YOU PLAY THIS FREE TIME LICK BY FEEL

Playing in and out of time

Tracks 51-52

There's no real rule here – it's all about the 'feel'. Simply speed up and slow down this repeating phrase as you see fit. Eventually you'll hit some rhythms that align with the rhythm of the backing music. It's a trick Jimi would often use in his improvised solos.

VIDEO RIFF LESSONS

Learn three classic Hendrix guitar riffs with our free video lessons on FileSilo

TG TIP
If you find thumb fretting uncomfortable, you can fret the sixth string with your first finger.

TG TIP
Find the sweet spot of your wah and use a smaller rocking motion, rather than the entire range of the pedal.

TG TIP
Select the neck pickup and roll off the volume and tone controls slightly to keep the tone mellow.

FOXEY LADY

Foxey Lady begins with a long, sustained F# note played at the 11th fret on the third string. Fret the note with your second finger, bunch your first finger up next to it to add support then increase your grip on the string. Add a wide vibrato, keeping your fingers locked in position and repeatedly turning your wrist back and forth, pulling the string in the direction of the floor. Try to generate a little feedback as your vibrato gets more intense. After sliding down the neck, form an unorthodox Fm7 chord shape with your thumb over the top of the neck, your third finger on the fourth string and your fourth finger barring the top two strings. The next chord is a B major, which lends the riff an F# Dorian flavour (F# G# A B C# D# E).

Cheat sheet
Appears at: 0:00-0:20
Tempo: 90bpm
Key/scale: F# Dorian
Main techniques: Wide vibrato and thumb fretting

VOODOO CHILD (SLIGHT RETURN)

There are two key playing elements to this classic guitar riff from 1968's *Electric Ladyland*. First up is the light shuffle groove, which you may not immediately pick up on because the swinging feel affects the 16th notes, rather than the more usual eighth notes in a shuffle rhythm. And, although you don't pick every note, you can match the shuffle groove to your downstrokes and upstrokes to keep your pick hand locked in time. The second vital part to master is Jimi's rhythmic wah phrases. Play a constant quarter note pulse on your wah's treadle – that means you press your toes down in time with the 85bpm tempo. The guitar on the recording is tuned down to E♭, but we've recorded our video in E standard so you can play along without retuning.

Cheat sheet
Appears at: 0:10-0:32
Tempo: 85bpm
Key/scale: E minor pentatonic
Main techniques: Wah wah / 16th note shuffle groove / string bends

THE WIND CRIES MARY

This riff is based on three chords, E♭, E and F, and these ascend the fretboard one fret at a time. Jimi plays the chords as 'inversions', which simply means the lowest note in the shape isn't the root – it's one of the other notes, instead. This method can make even the simplest chord sequence sound less predictable as the ear struggles to pick up on the root. On the first pass Jimi places the 5th intervals in the bass to give the chords a solid, fat sound. On the second time the chords are played with the major 3rds as the lowest notes and Jimi adds a hammer-on to each shape – a trademark of his rhythm style. Start by learning the chord shapes and making sure you can move cleanly from fret to fret. When you have the basics down you can try Jimi's hammer-on phrase. Watch the video for all the details.

Cheat sheet
Appears at: 0:00 -0:14
Tempo: 70bpm
Key/scale: Chromatic / E major
Main techniques: Chromatic chord movement and chord hammer-ons

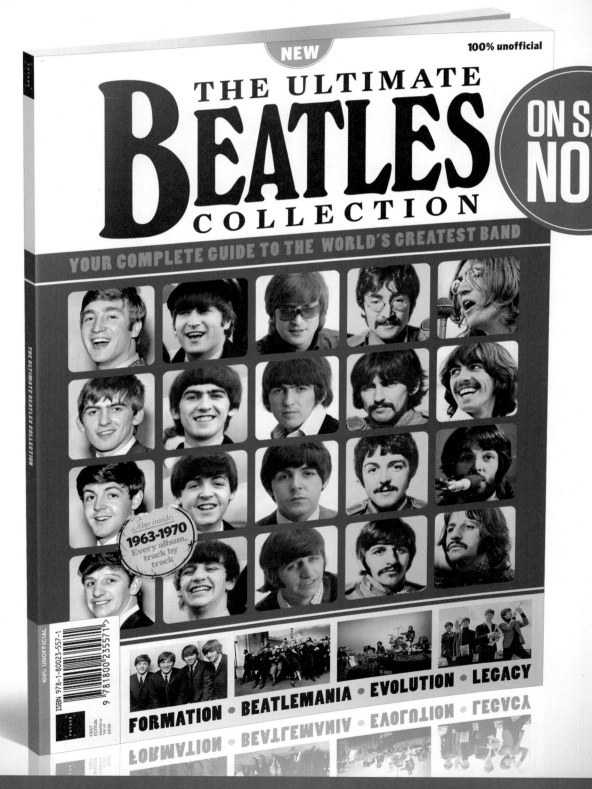

ERIC CLAPTON

From 1966 to 1976, Eric Clapton redefined the sound of rock guitar. Join us as we discover how this monumental decade changed the face of guitar playing forever…

The year was 1966. The year that saw Bob Dylan hold fast to his electric guitar with *Blonde On Blonde*; the year that saw FIFA World Cup madness drench England, and the year that celebrated the conviction of Moors Murderers Myra Hyndley and Ian Brady. London was well and truly swinging, with mini skirts, Mary Quant and Manfred Mann high on everyone's agendas. But from within the haze and smog of the big city grew an army of six-string fanatics, each preaching the word of 'god' and defacing public property with a single, immortal line: 'Clapton is God'. No exclamation marks were needed to punctuate the fervour of this statement. Nothing else needed to be said. Eric Clapton – barely entered into adulthood at 21 – had achieved deity status in the guitar world.

In a filthy underground station in Islington, London the first proclamation of Clapton's genius was sprayed-painted onto a wall. Scores more would soon follow elsewhere, and the phrase 'Clapton is God' became the new mantra for London's guitar-loving faithful.

After earning the nickname 'Slowhand' in The Yardbirds, Eric Clapton's guitar playing was legend by '66. Jimmy Page, peer, Led Zeppelin superstar and longtime friend of Clapton knew that whatever Clapton had, it was otherworldly. "When Eric was with The Bluesbreakers, it was a magical combination," he recalled. "He played brilliantly then, really brilliantly." Clapton's Yardbirds successor, Jeff Beck, admitted those were big shoes

he had to fill: "Back then we were both blues, and he was better."

Clapton's influence on rock guitar during his glory years was gargantuan. He played second fiddle to no-one, not even Hendrix. Think anything to the contrary? Let us set the record straight…

The well-worn story is that Jimi Hendrix led the 60s guitar pack. History hands him almost sole credit for making the electric six-string the most expressive musical instrument of our time. While we would never deny Hendrix of his rightful place as one of the most gifted players in the history of guitar, the late 60s were not just his possession. Not even close.

Much like Hendrix, Clapton grew up listening to rock 'n' roll and blues, reinventing the playing styles that came before him. Forget his later years, pock-marked by chart-humping tracks like *Wonderful Tonight* or the mournful *Tears In Heaven*: Clapton was, and will always be, a master of blues rock guitar. In John Mayall's Bluesbreakers, he honed his blues chops to enviable heights; with Cream he carved out a thick slab of heavy rock that's emulated to this day by millions of guitarists around the globe. From 1970 until the late 90s and beyond he poured out platinum release after platinum release, even revisiting some of his greatest tracks on the multi-Grammy-winning *Unplugged* because they were that good.

But it was from '66 to '76 that Clapton's star shone brighter than anyone else's. He embodied the vision of the ultimate guitar god, basking in the glory of his playing prowess and earning the respect and admiration of countless talented peers

"I was never into Hendrix like I was Clapton. I know every solo Clapton ever played, note for note"

EDDIE VAN HALEN

© Matt Gibbons

and future guitar stars. Ask Eddie Van Halen what turned him onto the guitar and he'll tell you straight: "It was the Bluesbreakers album with Eric Clapton on the front reading *The Beano* [John Mayall's Bluesbreakers With Eric Clapton]. I like Hendrix," says Eddie, "but I was never into him like I was Clapton. I know every solo Clapton ever played, note for note."

Much like EVH, Gary Moore cites the 'Beano album' as a major turning point in music: "It blew me away. I borrowed my friend's copy because I couldn't afford to buy it. I wore that out and scratched the shit out of it just learning the solos."

The 'Beano album' became a milestone in music. Having lodged with bluesman John Mayall, the 21-year-old Clapton immersed himself in Mayall's massive blues record collection and absorbed everything. As Clapton's soloing vocabulary shot light years ahead of his contemporaries', he also showed that white British musicians understood black American blues. The influences of his fast and fluent playing were clearly defined – BB, Freddie and Albert King, Buddy Guy and Otis Rush – but it was his fire, grit and passion that awoke a generation to a dangerous and exciting form of music that would remind them of the original blues artists that the world had all but forgotten.

By the time Hendrix arrived in Britain in September 1966, Clapton had already recorded 'Beano', quit Mayall and formed Cream with the

FROM FINGERSTYLE TO SLIDE, ERIC CLAPTON NAILS IT...

Many people think Clapton is a simple plectrum player or 'flat-picker'. But Eric's always used hybrid picking (pick and fingers) when he needs to and you can hear this on *Crossroads* from 1968's *Wheels Of Fire*.

As a slide player Clapton fused elements of George Harrison and Duane Allman. Listen to *Give Me Strength* from 1974's *461 Ocean Boulevard* for some cool slide guitar moments.

Acoustic-wise, Clapton's fingerstyle playing came to the fore on 1992's *Unplugged* album, and *Before You Accuse Me* is a great example of this.

nation's finest bassist and drummer, Jack Bruce and Ginger Baker. Their desire to play with Clapton was so strong that the famously feuding duo put their differences aside. While Clapton's Bluesbreakers playing was full of angst-ridden fury, in Cream it found maturity. The trio's almost instant success demanded a gruelling live schedule, which led to the band transforming their meagre repertoire into lengthy jams to fill time. This honed Clapton's skills to perfection: his solos became flowing and sophisticated, perfectly timed and building to frantic crescendos using a fat, crushing sound.

Clapton's Cream playing style has even made it into other guitarists' signature sounds, Texas-born rock virtuoso Eric Johnson's tone being a great demonstration: "I used to just sit and listen to the records and really study the way Clapton played, trying to get every inflection," Johnson remembers. "I was like an Eric Clapton jukebox for a couple of years."

In 1968, Beatles guitarist George Harrison persuaded Clapton to contribute a solo to a new Fab Four track: "[Clapton] said, 'Nobody plays on Beatles records,'" Harrison recalled. "I said, 'It's my song and I want you to play on it'. Anyway, Eric came in and played and it was really good." Many consider *While My Guitar Gently Weeps* from The Beatles' 'White' album to be one of Clapton's finest moments. In a single take, Clapton showed

CLAPTON-STYLE LICK 1: Bluesbreakers-style shuffle

The melodic grouping of two notes against the rhythmic grouping of three eighth notes during the pull-offs may throw you. Practise slowly, counting the beats.

CLAPTON-STYLE LICK 2: slow 60s blues

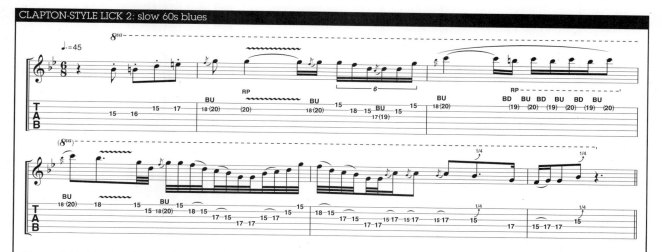

Fret the tone string bend in bar 3 at the 18th fret. Release the bend a little so that the pitch lowers by a semitone. These pitches are notated as (19) and (20).

CLAPTON-STYLE LICK 3: Strat blues

This is typical Clapton with phrases that dance around the beat. Try experimenting with the shorter phrases and make up your own.

"When Eric was with The Bluesbreakers it was a magical combination"

JIMMY PAGE

how dynamics and real bluesiness could fit into a pop classic.

That year Cream's differences tore the band apart, and in 1969 Eric put the short-lived Blind Faith together. The supergroup – made up of Traffic's Steve Winwood, Ric Grech of Family and Cream's own Ginger Baker – released just one album, and after one short tour they just fell apart.

Fed up with the limelight, Clapton hooked up with US husband-and-wife outfit Delaney and Bonnie Bramlett. It was here that Clapton took a much-needed back seat. His playing was changing. His cleaner-toned Stratocaster demanded a more laid-back approach with fewer notes and much less distortion, but his sophisticated touch remained, and it suited the country-flavoured music he was starting to enjoy.

When Clapton came to record his self-titled first solo album in 1970, he used the Bramletts' rhythm section, with Delaney producing. "Delaney brought something out of me that I didn't know I had," said Eric. Delaney and Bonnie's musicians – Bobby Whitlock on keys, drummer Jim Gordon and bassist Carl Radle – became the basis of Clapton's alter-ego band, Derek And The Dominos, who recorded their sole studio album, *Layla And Other Assorted Love Songs*, in a haze of mind-bending drugs, with Duane Allman on slide guitar. "He was like the musical brother I never had," confides Clapton. Allman repaid the compliment: "I was glad to have the opportunity to work with people of that magnitude, with that much brilliance and talent."

Although critically ignored, the album has since become a classic, and the title track – a cry of love to George Harrison's wife Pattie, who Clapton eventually married – contains one of the greatest rock riffs of all

---

CLAPTON'S TOP 5 TRACKS

Our pick of Clapton's finest guitar moments

HIDEAWAY (BLUESBREAKERS WITH CLAPTON)

Clapton set a Bluesbreakers precedent by recording this Freddie King instrumental that successors Peter Green and Mick Taylor would both follow. Eric rocks up this finger-twister with some fat Les Paul tone and blistering lead solos. In 1966 this was guitar technique on the edge.

HAVE YOU HEARD (BLUESBREAKERS WITH CLAPTON)

Clapton's greatest moment on the 'Beano album' sees the guitarist trading licks with tenor saxophonist Dick Heckstall-Smith. Eric builds up to his solo with tasty fills between the vocals before launching into one of the most kick-ass blues breaks that's ever been recorded.

I FEEL FREE (FRESH CREAM)

Packed full of riffs, rock track I Feel Free provides Clapton with the opportunity for a 'composed', un-bluesy solo. He begins on 'woman tone' (neck pickup on full, tone backed off) before switching to the bridge pickup for the solo's final lick.

CROSSROADS (WHEELS OF FIRE)

Arguably Clapton's finest track, this re-make of Robert Johnson's classic shows how Eric built the intensity of his live solos. There are two 24-bar breaks: the first is restrained and tasteful; the second takes off like a rocket, Eric throwing in everything he's got. Awesome!

LAYLA (LAYLA AND OTHER ASSORTED LOVE SONGS)

Written as a cry of love to Pattie Harrison, *Layla* launches into a multi-tracked riff in three octaves. Eric's sunburst Strat 'Brownie' screams out the tune, while guest Duane Allman's slide takes the song into the stratosphere. It's one of the greatest riffs of all time, no question.

A trade ad for Derek And The Dominos

From the There's One In Every Crowd Tour, 1975

Ginger Baker, Jack Bruce and Eric Clapton as Cream

In 2006 the Fender Custom Shop recreated Blackie with painstaking accuracy (pictured left)

ZUMA Press, Inc. / Alamy Stock Photo

Cream was the first rock supergroup

Pictorial Press Ltd / Alamy Stock Photo

"I scratched the shit out Mayall's 'Beano album' learning to play the solos"

GARY MOORE

GOD'S GEAR
THE SETUP THAT GAVE ERIC HIS LEGENDARY SOUND...

Clapton's Bluesbreakers setup was a Marshall 50-watt combo and '60 Gibson Les Paul. In Cream he used a JTM45 100-watt half-stack in the studio and stacked two amps on four 4x12 cabinets onstage. When his Les Paul was stolen, Clapton switched to a '64 ES-335 and an early 60s SG. During his solo career Fender Strats (vintage or Custom Shop 'signatures') have been favourite, with Soldano, Cornell and vintage tweed Fender Twin amplifiers.

time. *Layla And Other Assorted Love Songs* showed the world a sharper-toned, more pop-oriented Clapton, his Strat maintaining that lighter edge. That same year, Hendrix died, never knowing The Dominos had covered of one of his greatest songs, *Little Wing*.

Hendrix's unexpected death fuelled Clapton's mounting depression and increasing reliance on drugs. After several years in a heroin-induced recluse, Clapton emerged clean in 1974. His first album after recovery, *461 Ocean Boulevard*, breathed an understated class with songs like *Let It Grow* and *Give Me Strength*, featuring Harrison/Allman-influenced slide guitar. The album's surprise hit, though, was a cover of Bob Marley's *I Shot The Sheriff*. As a result of Clapton's patronage, Marley's career received a huge boost. "To my utter astonishment it went straight to No 1,"

declared Clapton. "I didn't meet Bob Marley until much later, but he did call me up when the single came out and seemed pretty happy."

Many Cream-era Clapton followers hated the new laid-back Eric. But despite the hecklers, this easy style was garnering new fans and when Slowhand covered JJ Cale's *Cocaine*, it struck a chord in both camps. *Cocaine*'s insistent riff propelled the track along and Clapton's glossy, Stratocaster-toned playing showed confidence and maturity, eschewing the need for flashy speed.

Eric Clapton's career has lasted 40 years beyond Cream. It's one of the greatest in all of rock, and the fact that it was founded on playing blues guitar is a testament to Clapton's dedication to his music and influences. His playing continues to evolve, and today's Clapton is an accomplished acoustic finger-stylist, a fine slide player, and his blues lead lines remain recognisable from one single phrase.

As BB King puts it: "I've been around the world and met kings and queens, but I've never met a more gracious man than Eric Clapton. In my opinion, Clapton's No 1." Clapton is God.

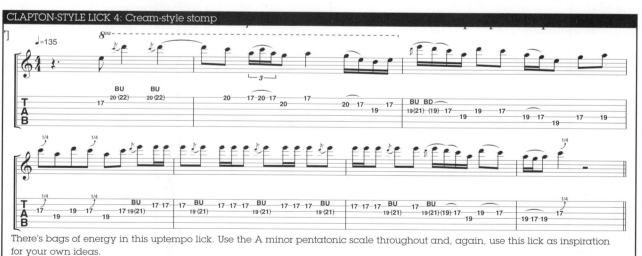

CLAPTON-STYLE LICK 4: Cream-style stomp

There's bags of energy in this uptempo lick. Use the A minor pentatonic scale throughout and, again, use this lick as inspiration for your own ideas.

THE RED STRATOCASTER

For thousands of guitarists in the early 60s, a Fiesta Red Fender Stratocaster symbolised a thrilling new era of music. Hank Marvin was the first iconic exponent of the red Strat, coaxing clean tones as lush as a manicured lawn from his famous Fender, but a hard-charging generation of players that followed found the Strat could scream as well as sigh – and the late, great Gary Moore was one of the finest among them. His '61 Fiesta Red Strat is synonymous with his blistering blues-rock style – while the origin of its distinctive milky-red finish, which is not a factory Fiesta Red, still holds mysteries. When Fender released an exacting Custom Shop replica of Gary's famous guitar in 2016, to mark the fifth anniversary of his death, we joined his tech, Graham Lilley, to hear tales of Moore's favourite solidbody. Here is the resulting story, first published when the replica was launched...

When *Guitarist* reported on the auction of the late, great Gary Moore's guitar collection, one comment that came back from readers was: 'Nice, but where's the Red Strat?' Like Clapton's lost 'Beano' 'Burst or Larry Carlton's '68 ES-335, some instruments are indelibly associated with a player. Even though Gary Moore used a very wide variety of guitars during the fiery course of his career, it is to the Fiesta Red '61 Stratocaster that many of his fans return, again and again, as an icon of his artistry. So when we learned that Fender Custom Shop Master Builder John Cruz [who has since left Fender] had been given the green light to build an exacting replica of Gary's Red Strat – also known as the Pink Strat, for reasons that shall become clear – we couldn't turn down the opportunity to investigate further. At the event (made possible thanks to the help

of Gary's former tech Graham Lilley, who is now custodian of Moore's extensive collection of gear), we were privileged to be able to examine the well-worn original and place it side by side with John Cruz's lovingly crafted replica for close comparison. Plug it in and crank up the volume? No problem, says Graham. If there was ever a feature likely to keep us staying happily in the office *After Hours*, this is it...

But before we arrived at that bit, we sat down with Graham to hear the story of how Gary came to own the iconic guitar in the first place, and what role it eventually played in his sonic arsenal. Graham begins by explaining that it very nearly didn't reach Gary's hands at all, as it was reportedly earmarked for sale to prog legend Greg Lake of Emerson, Lake & Palmer. "I wasn't there myself, but it was during the recording of the *Greg Lake* album in '81," Graham explains. "As usual with these things, there are variations on the story. I always understood that a chap turned up at the rehearsals, or to

"Greg Lake turns up, has a look at it, and Gary said he had his fingers crossed thinking, 'Please don't buy it. Please don't buy it.' After a bit of deliberation Greg passed on it, because it was maybe just a little bit too beaten up for his tastes..." GRAHAM LILLEY

the studio, with a couple of guitars. Gary was there and he was sold one first. It was an ES-5, which Gary either bought straight off or bought from Greg, when Greg didn't want it. Gary also tried the Strat and even just acoustically was like, 'Oh my God, it's incredible. I haven't even plugged it in.' But the deal was that it was there just for Greg to have a look at. But Gary was like, 'Just listen to that.' He knew that if it was that resonant acoustically, when you plug it in it is just going to be louder isn't it?

"So Greg turns up, has a look at it. Gary said he had his fingers crossed thinking, 'Please don't buy it. Please don't buy it.' After a bit of deliberation Greg passed on it, because it was maybe just a little bit too beaten up for his tastes. Obviously not as beaten up as it is now – but it wasn't totally pristine even then. So Gary was like: 'Right, that's mine.' That was it: the deal was done.

"Gary had it from then on," Graham continues. "He did most of *Corridors Of Power* with it and he was playing it a lot live, around that time. Then it was on pretty much most of the next album – *Victims Of The Future* – and sporadically from then on. Then it went missing on its way to America. Whether it disappeared in this country, or strayed when it arrived in America, no-one is sure. But somehow it resurfaced somewhere in Texas. At any rate, it was found and sent back. But by then, Gary had bought two '62 Fender reissues off-the-peg – a white one and a sunburst one. We've still got one of those, which is now [refinished in] pale blue.

"I'm not sure if that was the sunburst one or if that was the white one, because there were two and they both changed colours. One did become very flamingo pink at one point. We won't talk about that one – it was too pink! It was Barbie pink, beyond Barbie. That's long gone as well. But the red '61 Strat was part of his armoury pretty much ever since really – but most notably, when he played a cover of *Red House* for Fender's 50th anniversary of the Strat gig. I think that goes down in history as one of the greatest performances of that song ever. I just remember looking round at people's faces after he did the first solo. It was just like, 'What happened? Did the Queen walk in?'"

Close scrutiny of Gary's famous Strat reveals that it is not in anything like original condition, and Graham says it was likely to have been a hard-working professional instrument even before Gary bought it, with all the maintenance and upgrades that usually entails.

"It was refretted quite early on. Just jogging back slightly, the supposed history of the guitar was that it came from the sideman in Tommy Steele's band, although I cannot find out anything about him. And obviously, it had been resprayed and refinished at some point. What was it originally? John Cruz of Fender's Custom Shop wasn't certain, but he said with the kind of yellow primer base that's visible in places it could have been Sunburst originally. To confuse matters further, the top coat of 'Fiesta' red paint is lighter than another coat of red finish that's visible underneath."

Here we stray back into the long-running debate about the so-called 'Selmer' refinishes, which were purportedly applied to Strats of various factory finishes imported in Britain in the early 60s, then resprayed in an ersatz 'Fiesta Red' because so many players of the era wanted to imitate Hank Marvin.

At this point *Guitar Techniques* editor Neville Marten, who jammed with Gary many times, chimes in with his recollections of working at Fender's UK guitar repair workshop in the early 80s, when many such instruments passed through his hands.

"Everyone who worked in guitar repair in that era knows there were Strats that can only be described as pink and not red. Loads of them were later refinished white because of Hendrix eventually replacing Hank as the guitarist people wanted to be like. But what you found if you went to refinish them again is you couldn't get that pink paint off because it was like *rock*. It was the colour of Lifebuoy Soap as well. That was how we all described it."

While it's impossible to say if Gary's '61 Strat is one such guitar, as Graham points out you can clearly see that a thin, milky-red finish has been sprayed onto a darker coat of red paint underneath. A British respray to 'faux Fiesta' spec

---

FIRST PLAY

Neville Marten on the first time Gary passed him the Red Strat – and why its neck profile remains its most stunning feature

"The first time I saw this guitar was in a hotel room in London with Gary and Graham [Lilley]", recalls *Guitar Techniques* editor and *Guitarist* contributor Neville Marten, who interviewed and jammed with Gary many times over the years and came to know him quite well. "One funny detail was that I turned up and Gary was wearing a denim shirt. I walked in and he said, 'Fucking hell, Neville. I put a denim shirt on especially, because you always wear denim.' Instead, I was wearing some poncy white shirt with black spots on it, which spoiled his joke – he liked to take the piss out of me, although always in a good-humoured way. By coincidence, I got up this morning and, without thinking about it, put a denim shirt on to come here and play Gary's Strat again, so that's fitting in a way!

"Anyway, going back to the day I first encountered this guitar, Gary was sitting on the sofa with the Strat and he said, 'Do you want to play it?', which of course I did and he passed it to me. I put my hand around the neck and it instantly struck me then, as it always has since, that it was the best Strat neck I have ever held in my hands. I always think about that when I imagine the perfect Strat – because it had that seemingly wide-ish nut. With some guitars you seem to have acres of room on the fretboard and with others your fingers seemed more cramped. It could be to the tune of half a millimetre or what have you, but it seems to make all the difference. People talk about the [slender] '63-shaped neck... I think Gary's Strat is getting towards that, but it might even be shallower, plus it's had 40-odd years of wear and tear on it [In fact, when building the replica, the Fender Master Builder John Cruz found that the original radius had tangibly flattened off due to playing-wear – Ed]. I was also struck by the fact that Gary's '61 Strat had a very, very dark rosewood 'board. But they all did in those days, didn't they?"

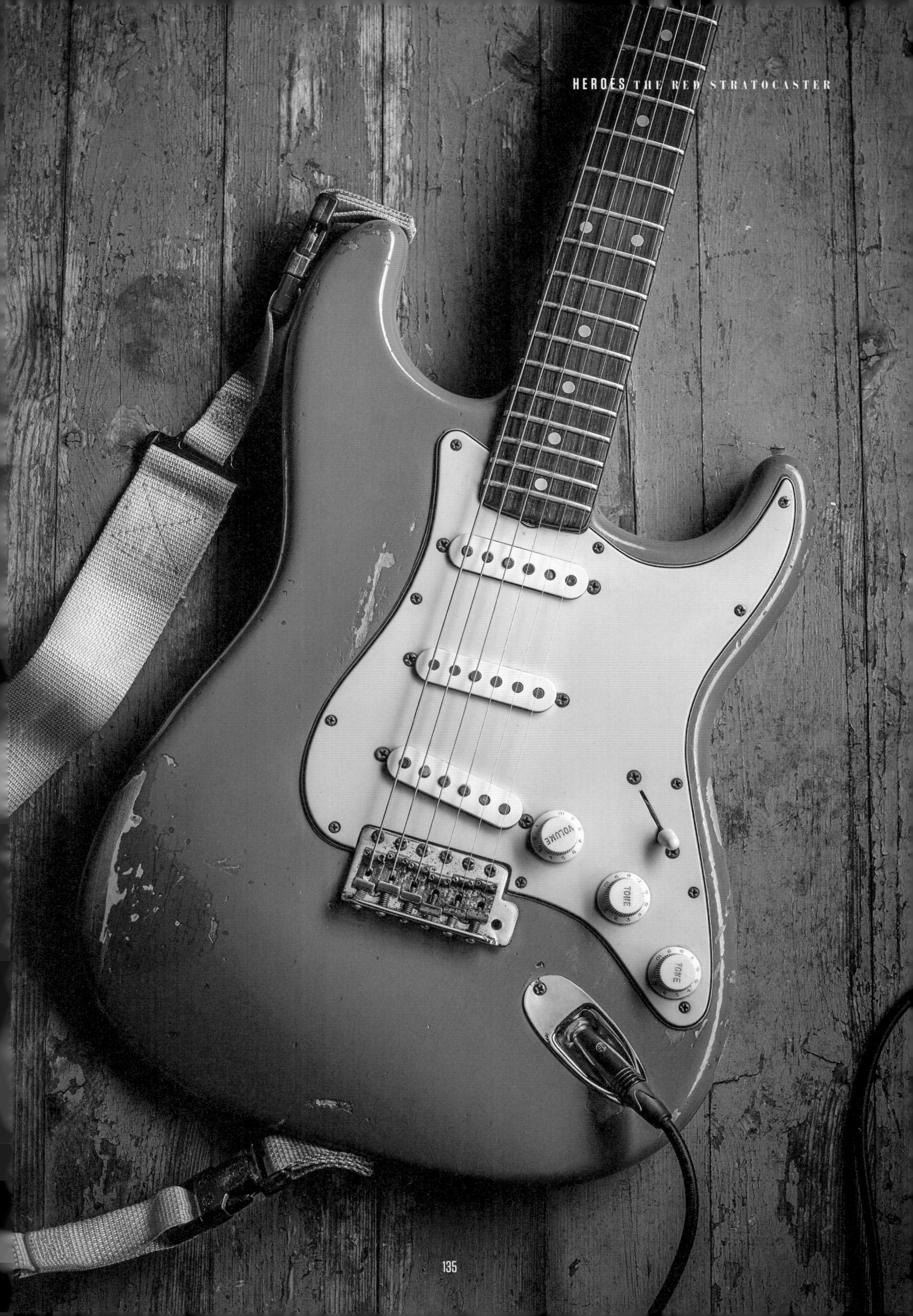
VOLUME
TONE
TONE

"Gary was pretty on the money. He hit the notes he meant to hit – and they stayed hit. It was the right note at the right time, generally" GRAHAM LILLEY

over an original Dakota Red? Perhaps, but there is no way to be sure. Similarly, the neck and middle pickups are also non-original. Graham explains that, like many hardware changes made on the road, the pickup alterations were wholly pragmatic.

"They just needed redoing. Obviously, when some parts broke they had to be swapped out. For example, we were doing the *A Different Beat* album back in 1998 and the neck pickup went, so I posted it up to Seymour Duncan. He rewound it and sent it back, popped it in and was like, 'Great. Let's go.' Then the middle pickup went in the middle of the *Monsters Of Rock* tour in 2003 at Wembley. I had an old Duncan Antiquity pickup that was sat in a box and just threw that in. But then he didn't use [the Strat] for a quite while. Well, he used it a bit on the *Power Of The Blues* album in 2004. Then it was on a few bits of the last three albums, *Old New Ballads Blues*, *Close As You Get* and *Bad For You Baby*. But the Telecaster was probably used more on a lot of those things.

"All the same, I eventually got Tim Mills at Bare Knuckle pickups to rewind the original broken middle pickup, which is still in the case, and not in the guitar, at present. Another thing I did, when it proved necessary, was take the rear-most tone pot, which obviously didn't get used that much, and moved that up to replace the volume when that went. I then filled the gap it left with a newer, replacement tone pot. That way you still had that sort of vintage feel because an original part had just been moved up a place."

The neck, too – which has a slender, shallow C-profile that graduates smoothly and organically into the diminutive headstock with no apparent step or volute to the flat rear surface of the headstock – saw some pragmatic updates made to it, including refretting with chunky wire to suit Gary's needs.

"It was the biggest wire that Dunlop did at the time, the 6100. Which might upset a few purists, but it works, you know? The intonation would be pretty good on it, because the frets were such a solid lump, you know? So they certainly worked. When it came to the acoustic resonance off the top of [each note]... you would just get even more. But Gary was pretty on the money. He hit the notes he meant to hit – and they stayed hit. It was the right note at the right time, generally."

As the images attest, Gary's '61 Strat bears the battlescars of his high-intensity performances. How much of the heavy wear visible on the Red Strat was put there by Gary in the course of his career, we ask?

"Quite a bit. I was going back through old photographs. It is very noticeable," Graham adds.

1. A thin, milky-red post-factory finish is clearly visible over a darker-red coat of paint beneath it, with off-white primer beneath that, hinting at a possible British refinish early on in the guitar's life

2. The finish on the rear of the guitar is extensively scoured away by years of use in Gary's hands

3. The neck pickup was rewound by Seymour Duncan in 1998, while the original broken pickup from the middle position was eventually rewound by Bare Knuckle Pickups. A Seymour Duncan Antiquity is installed on the guitar, however

4. The bridge pickup is the only remaining original pickup installed on the guitar today

5. The headstock, bearing a much-darkened spaghetti Fender logo, is quite dainty

6. Three springs were Gary's preference for vibrato setup, though Graham says Gary often used the guitar with vibrato arm removed

7. As with the pickups, pots have been replaced

LEGACY OF LOUD

The recorded voice of the Red Strat is well known to Gary's fans, but it was used with a very wide variety of amplification, as Moore was a restless experimenter with tone, as Graham Lilley explains.

"Gary used the Red Strat with a variety of amps. It was his 1959 100-watt Super Lead Marshalls to begin with, four-input jobs. And also 50-watt Marshall 1987s in various shapes and sizes – big boxes, small boxes – in various vintages. But then he used all sorts of stuff. Like on the *Scars* album he was going through Marshalls and Fender Tonemasters on a couple of occasions.

"The Strat also got used on *Still Got The Blues* on *Too Tired*, a track he did with Albert Collins and it's the slide on *Moving On*, even though for live we used a different guitar – a bog-standard Squier Strat – but it's on the video, and that would be through the Soldano SLO100 with the EV 412s, so there's another colouration to it.

"But there was also those little Plexi combos he got off Denis Cornell. We were using a couple of those things, little 2x12 Vibroverb '62 reissues got used. There was also a 'blackface' 1963 Fender Twin on parts of the *King Of The Blues* track on the *Still Got The Blues* CD. There was a Prosonic that got tried for a couple of things. Mostly studio, not live because obviously those small combos wouldn't quite cut it. Then there was an anniversary Marshall – not the

1. The neck of the '61 original blends smoothly and organically into the headstock – recalling guitarist Jim Campilongo's pithy observation that this fragile but elegant point of transition on vintage Fenders resembles "an old lady's wrist". The neck is stamped November '60

2. As mentioned, the neck and middle pickups of Gary's '61 Strat are not in original condition, but the bridge pup is. The DC resistance readings are 6.5k (neck), 5.9k (middle) and 5.3k (bridge)

3. Original and volume pots have either been replaced outright as needed or moved up by one slot to fill a gap left by the removal of a faulty original

HOW THEY COMPARE

Our initial impressions of these two glorious guitars plugged in

Given the uniqueness of Gary's Strat and the scarcity of the new John Cruz replica, we were privileged to be able to get both in the same room to make a plugged-in comparison, playing through a Gear Of The Year-winning Fender '57 Custom Tweed Twin. Our test pilot was Neville Marten, who had already played Gary's Red Strat around 10 years ago. Here's what Nev had to say about how the two guitars compare: "They are very similar in weight – there isn't an obvious difference in that regard. The neck on the '61 has worn totally smooth, however. It's like running our fingers over silk. To say you can 'feel edges' on the replica is not correct, because it's been aged and fettled very skillfully, but 40 years of playing means there isn't the faintest suggestion of a hard edge or even a corner or anything, anywhere on Gary's Strat.

"Sonically, the reissue was a touch more powerful – it went into natural feedback and sustain quicker than Gary's did, which could be a plus if that's what you're after. But crucially, the tonal similarity between the two guitars is definitely there. Both played really great and there was no significant difference in that regard.

"In conclusion, the replica is a stunning piece of work and a superb guitar in its own right. The ageing was incredibly accurate, and while you could produce a micrometer and find small differences here and there, I would never, ever feel short-changed by the essential accuracy – leaving aside one or two deliberate differences such as the pickups, as the poles have a different stagger on the replica. As for Gary's '61, I would count it among the top three or four Strats I've ever played. And, weirdly, Gary's natural-finish 'bitsa' one that I played in issue 403 was one of the other great Strats I've played! He could certainly pick a good one!"

To hear the difference yourself, check out Nev's video demo at: http://bit.ly/guitaristextra

4. The headstock of the replica is superbly aged, though if we're splitting hairs, it looks to be fractionally larger than that of the original

5. Detailing includes a recreation of Gary's quick-release DiMarzio ClipLock strap

6. The milky, thin refinish over a darker (possibly Dakota Red) original finish has been carefully emulated on John Cruz's Master Built replica

"He would use wildly different guitars, from Strats to Teles to Les Pauls to 335s, Gretsches, even... yet he could make it all sound good"
NEVILLE MARTEN

Silver Jubilee, but a thing they did later, which was celebrating Jim Marshall's 85th birthday, the 1923C. It was a great-sounding combo – the sound was a variation of the DSL50, but it was slightly different. They were quite good. And then live was another thing: when we did the *After The War* tour back in '89 we had 400 watts of Marshalls literally all the way upon stage!"

Neville Marten additionally observes that "all that goes to show he would use wildly different guitars, from Strats to Teles to Les Pauls to 335s, Grestches even... And he'd be playing them into all those different amps of different powers based on 6V6s, EL34s, 6L6s... yet he could make it all sound good because of what was coming out of the muscles in his fingers and his brain."

"And his heart," Graham Lilley interjects.

"Yes, and his heart," Neville continues adding that, for Gary, picking up a guitar had a transformational effect. "If he was sitting in a room and talking just like we are around this table, and you stuck a guitar in his hand it would be like flicking a switch. You could say he turned from David Banner into the Incredible Hulk as soon as you put a guitar in his hand... he suddenly became this hugely powerful ox-like presence that was undefeatable – and he was. Nobody would take Gary on in guitar in any contest. Not that he was thinking that way."

"The guitar was almost like his armour," Graham Lilley concurs. "In some ways he was very shy and a little awkward. People say, 'Really?' when I tell them that, but yes, he was very shy. He put that Strat on and it was a buffer between him and the rest of the world, and he could just express himself through that."

CUSTOMS BARRIER
Gary's '61 Strat has a special place in the hearts of many of his fans, for obvious reasons, but in and of itself, it's a guitar that resonates with many British players particularly, given that a Fiesta Red Strat (refinished or otherwise) of this vintage encapsulates the boyhood aspirations of so many Hank Marvin-inspired players. So it seems an obvious subject for a Fender Custom Shop replica – nonetheless, the project was to have a lengthy gestation period, as Graham Lilley explains.

"I'd been having a conversation with John Cruz from Fender's Custom Shop for a good while – 20 or more years. Probably longer now, actually, because Gary has been gone six years come February. So it was

prior to that. We sort of kept in touch and discussed it and John, being a huge fan of Gary's, had always wanted to do something, whether it was a special order someone was asking for or something, he wanted to do this model one day. I think, initially, he couldn't get it past head office, because Gary wasn't quite a household name in America. Among guitar players, obviously... For us, it is a different case. But the average man on the street might only remember him from an episode of *Top Of The Pops* standing next to Phil [Lynott]. So for a while, there was a wait to get the Custom Shop management on side, to make it attractive as a worthwhile project. Obviously, in certain quarters of the globe it would have been snapped up very readily – here, or in Japan or Germany especially. But John and I kept in touch and sent ideas back and forth via fax. This goes back a long way – to transatlantic phone calls and so on. It'd be like, 'What do you need? I have got this vinyl or this picture of it, if it helps?' And so on. So we just had this ongoing conversation.

"Eventually, John said, 'I think we can move forward on it. Let me see if I can get the green light on this.' Then he said, 'Yes, I am going to come over. Let's have a look at it and see what we can do. We will spend a day carefully taking it apart, measuring it, taking photos, getting the colour right.' So we did that last May. As I say, he came over early April this year with a prototype and went back. He went on to take the prototype to the Gary Moore Memorial Concert in Budapest, and played it on stage with the house band as part of the evening's concert."

MASTER STROKE

At this point, the story shifts back in time and West in location to Fender's Custom Shop headquarters in Corona, California, which *Guitarist* visited back in July. While we were there, we chatted with veteran Master Builder John Cruz who actually had the prototype of the replica Gary Moore Stratocaster featured in this article sitting on his workbench at that time. Tellingly, the tricky-to-nail milky-red finish was set to undergo a further revision before production, after careful A/B analysis of minute paint-chips from the original guitar revealed a slight darkening would be necessary to provide an exact match. As John was one of the Custom Shop's most experienced builders and a huge Gary

Moore fan, we asked how much of a labour of love the project had been – and what efforts he'd made to evoke both the spirit and the detail of the original in his Master Built replica instrument.

"We went out to London to take a look at the guitar and Graham Lilley brought the guitar in and I sat down with him. I was particularly nervous about it, just seeing it for the first time since I saw him last. I got to see it; I got all shaky, man, it's like, 'Jesus, there it is' and it was really wonderful to have the opportunity to examine it up close, and take it all apart. I got pictures and video and everything.

"For example, it has a lot of really weird neck-wear that I've never seen on any guitar before – it has these black things on it and I'm not actually exactly sure what that was, but I replicated it, right down to the grain of the wood and density and everything. I do kind of wish they would have let me have the guitar to work on it here, though. Like, I had Rory Gallagher's guitar here for four months. So I got to make the prototype one-to-one with the guitar and it was identical. But, all the same, the Gary Moore Strat is pretty much spot on."

Although the pickups on the replica have a different stagger to those on the original, they are carefully voiced to match the sound of the original, says John.

"The pickups on Gary's guitar were on the low side, output-wise, as Strats go and a couple of pickups have been rewound. So are we going to go to that extent? Probably not. So I had a set custom-wound here, matching those readings that I got and they're basically my pickups. They're things that I use already. They're similarly low-output pickups – which I swear by now. I used to be one of those guys who was like, 'The higher the [DC resistance] readings the better. More output. But now I've kind of turned around – the lower output pickups, that's the real deal. It's clean. It sounds great. You put an overdrive on it, it's just going to explode and come alive."

The results can be judged overleaf, in Dave Burrluck's review of John's exacting replica, and heard on our accompanying video on our YouTube channel. While such guitars are produced in prohibitively small numbers and at a price that excludes most players, all 50 of the run of Gary Moore Strats have already been sold – testament to John's obsessive attention to the craft of replication, which he says is his natural calling as a guitar maker.

"I never got to see the original SRV Number One. It was a project that was supposed to go to [Senior Master Builder] John English, but he was too busy at the time to do it and that's when [former Custom Shop head] Mike Eldred came to me. He said, 'What do you think about doing this?' and he showed me the pictures and I'm like, 'Give me that' and I grabbed the body and the neck, and I ran through paint and I made a prototype and then we showed it to Jimmie Vaughan and he signed off on it. So I knew that was going to be my niche – doing one-to-one replicas – and so that's how it's been ever since."

ABOVE As you'd expect for such an expensive replica, there's a fair bit of case candy here – plus the heavy-duty flightcase itself

OPPOSITE Former Master Builder John Cruz, pictured at his workbench in Fender's Custom Shop in 2016. In his arms is a prototype of the Gary Moore replica Strat featured here

FENDER GARY MOORE STRAT

It might be a slavish repro of the late, great man's Stratocaster, but here we ask the question, as a new guitar at £8,000, how does Fender's Limited Edition Gary Moore Stratocaster really stack up?

All Strats are the same, right? If only. It's a testament to the design of this all-time classic that models of a similar price level can sound, play and feel, remarkably different. You find a good one then, dammit, you play another that trumps it. Throw in the diverse range of styles that the Strat has excelled in, in the hands of a diverse number of players, and you have a seemingly simple instrument that can be annoyingly slippery to define.

So with just 27 of these £8k Gary Moore tributes coming to Europe, how does it fit into this world? This writer was dispatched to Fender's Artist centre at John Henry's rehearsal complex, with no knowledge of Gary's original Strat, to take a look.

As we examine the guitar we notice the enhanced contours with different colour undercoats – both white and a yellow – plus, on the forearm contour, the darker Dakota Red shows through the Fiesta Red. The neck wear is interesting, too, in that although it's worn away on the treble and bass side, there's visible lacquer on the centre back – another indicator that many 'heavy' relics really aren't that accurate: this is a replica of a guitar that has obviously been played at a high pro-level. The wear on the rear of the guitar not only approximates the original, but looks very real. It's a convincing piece.

Some players might be surprised at its relatively thin neck depth in lower positions, which fills out up the neck and measures 19.4mm at the 1st fret and 22.8mm at the 12th. Of course, some of that might be down to the flattening of the original's fingerboard radius over the numerous refrets – it would have been 7.25 inches originally; now it's spec'd at 10 inches – which obviously slightly reduces the neck depth.

There's a typically 'old' ring and resonance to the acoustic voice; the vibrato is set with three springs and approximately one tone upbend on the G string. We'd taken along our well-used Road Worn Strat as our reference and, as you'd perhaps expect, the Gary Moore has a noticeably more vibrant response.

Now, DC resistance readings aren't the best indication of what's happening with the pickups, but here we measured the bridge at 5.76k ohms, the middle at 6.03k and the neck at 5.78k, far from the modern thinking of a 'graduated' set where, typically, the bridge is the hottest. And plugged in, the bridge really has quite a low-output, edgy sound that's beautifully contrasted by the neck pickup. The surprise, perhaps, is the close voicing of the neck and middle pickups; for example, through a crunchy, gained Bassbreaker on lower-string voicings, the difference is minimal, but past the 12th fret lead lines on the top strings sound *profoundly* different.

The appeal then, from a new guitar standpoint, is this tonal width and contrast – each pickup has its own character and nuance and there's a sweetness to the bridge that sounds edgy and wiry, but far from weedy. Also, the pickup heights are a little different from how many of us would set them: the bridge, as set, has virtually no tilt – it's approximately 2mm from the strings (fretted at the top fret) on both treble and bass sides, while the middle pickup is, despite it's beefiest DC reading, set the closest to the strings, again with relatively little tilt.

To a collector and/or Gary Moore fanatic, it's probably worth the cost, although we struggle to justify that kind of money without the guitar's back-story. It is, however, one of the most realistic Relics we've played; the attention to the smallest details is impressive, not to mention its 'old guitar' resonance and feel. But it's the pickups and sounds that intrigue us: that low-output bridge pickup really works, adding subtle and very wide dynamic range to the instrument.

VERDICT

It can be a depressing experience to play a guitar as good as this (not least because our own go-to Strat now feels and sounds inferior in comparison). We might not be able to stretch up to a Master Built any time soon, but this guitar's pickup specs, settings and three-way pickup switch have given us plenty to think about on the way home. Like we say, not all Strats are created equal!

TECH SPEC

PRICE: £8,000
BODY: 2-piece offset seam lightweight alder
NECK: Maple, custom Oval 'C' profile, bolt-on
SCALE LENGTH: 648mm (25.5")
NUT/WIDTH: Bone/41.9mm
FINGERBOARD: Select dark African blackwood, 254mm (10") radius
FRETS: 21, jumbo
HARDWARE: Aged nickel-plated American Vintage vibrato, Fender vintage-style tuners
STRING SPACING, BRIDGE: 55mm
ELECTRICS: 3x Custom Shop John Cruz-designed Bone-Tone single coils, 3-position lever pickup selector switch, master volume, tone 1 (neck), tone 2 (middle)
WEIGHT (kg/lb): 3.6/8
FINISHES: Colour-matched Fiesta Red custom Relic nitro lacquer (body), Custom Relic tinted nitro lacquer (neck)

The John Cruz Master Built Gary Moore Stratocaster is a thing of beauty, though its price is prohibitively high for most players

Celebrate the songs and sounds of the greatest decades in music

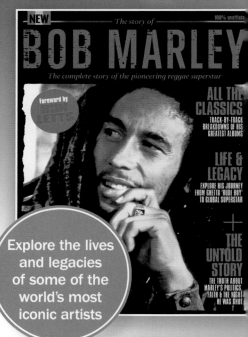

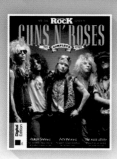

Explore the lives and legacies of some of the world's most iconic artists

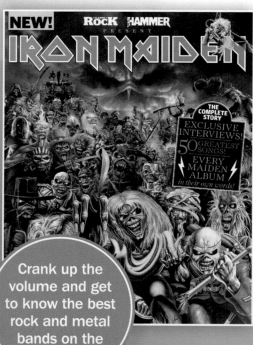
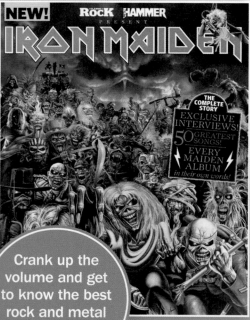

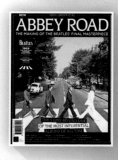

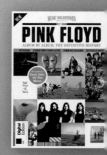

Crank up the volume and get to know the best rock and metal bands on the planet

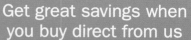

Get great savings when you buy direct from us

1000s of great titles, many not available anywhere else

World-wide delivery and super-safe ordering

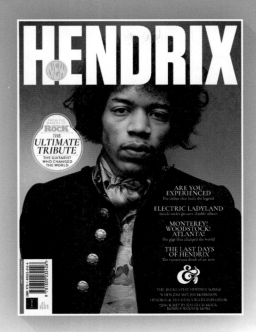

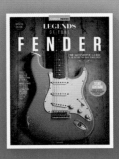

★CLASSIC★ ROCK

HIGH VOLTAGE ⚡ ROCK'N'ROLL

www.classicrockmagazine.com